Walk

HISTORIC
DEVON

Walks in
HISTORIC
DEVON

MICHAEL BENNIE

COUNTRYSIDE BOOKS

NEWBURY, BERKSHIRE

First published 2001
© Michael Bennie 2001

COUNTRYSIDE BOOKS
3 Catherine Road
Newbury, Berkshire

To view our complete range of books,
please visit us at
www.countrysidebooks.co.uk

ISBN 1 85306 680 X

Designed by Graham Whiteman
Maps by Michael Bennie and redrawn by Philippa Gillatt
Photographs by the author

Produced through MRM Associates Ltd, Reading
Printed by J.W. Arrowsmith Ltd, Bristol

Contents

AREA MAP SHOWING LOCATION OF THE WALKS

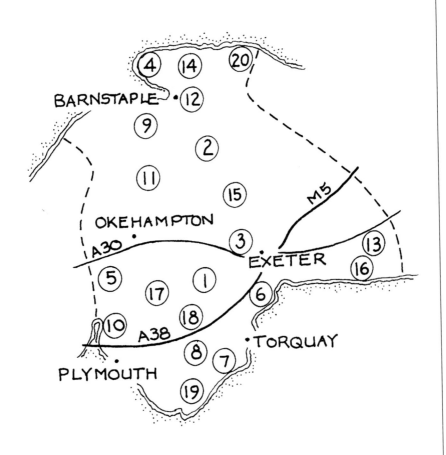

WALK

PUBLISHER'S NOTE

We hope that you obtain considerable enjoyment from this book; great care has been taken in its preparation. Although at the time of publication all routes followed public rights of way or permitted paths, diversion orders can be made and permissions withdrawn.

We cannot, of course, be held responsible for such diversion orders and any inaccuracies in the text which result from these or any other changes to the routes nor any damage which might result from walkers trespassing on private property. We are anxious though that all details covering the walks are kept up to date and would therefore welcome information from readers which would be relevant to future editions.

Introduction

From Bronze Age settlements to 20th century monuments, evidence of the history of Devon lies all around us, just waiting to be discovered. And the twenty walks in this book aim to help you uncover that history, while also exploring some of the most attractive areas of this beautiful county.

There are events that changed the course of history; but there are also stories with a purely local significance – accounts of persecution, kindness, perseverance, crimes and rivalries which hardly touched the national consciousness. There are tales of great men and small, of saints, rogues and eccentrics, of merchants and seamen, all of them associated with a particular site which can be visited and which will hopefully breathe life into the dry historical record. If you would like to investigate any aspect of this history in more detail, there is a short bibliography at the end of the book which lists some of the publications I found most interesting and useful during my researches.

Devon is a county of diverse landscapes, and the areas through which the walks take you are as varied as the history they represent. Rugged cliffs and sandy beaches, barren expanses of moorland and rich farmland, rolling hills and deep wooded valleys, large rivers and small streams – all are represented, as well as a few urban streets and alleys.

The walks are circular, and either start at the chosen site or take you to it. They range in length from 2¼ to 7½ miles, and both route descriptions and sketch maps are provided. If you want more detail, the numbers of the relevant Ordnance Survey sheets are provided. The Landranger maps cover a greater area, but at a scale of 1:50,000 are less detailed than the 1:25,000 Outdoor Leisure or Explorer series. The latter are ideal for walkers. They show field boundaries, byways, etc, which can be invaluable if you are not quite sure of your route; and in some built-up areas a greater level of detail is a great advantage. I have, however, tried to make the directions as clear as possible, so you should hopefully only need the OS maps if you are planning to extend your walk or deviate from the route provided.

For each circuit, I have indicated where I would recommend stopping off for refreshments. I hope you agree with the choices, while accepting that they are based on my own personal preferences. And, of course, you should be aware that menus – and indeed proprietors – change from time to time so, although the information provided is accurate to the best of my knowledge, I have provided telephone numbers so that you can check for yourselves whether a particular hostelry suits your needs. Most of these establishments are actually on the route, but in a few cases they may require a short detour. The pubs mentioned are generally quite happy for customers to leave cars in their car parks while they walk, but please do ask before doing so.

I have thoroughly enjoyed delving into the hidden corners of Devon's history and exploring areas of the county I had not come across before. My hope is that you will get the same enjoyment from the results of my researches.

Michael Bennie

WALK 1
BRONZE AGE LIFE – GRIMSPOUND
Length: 3½ miles

A hut circle, Grimspound

HOW TO GET THERE: The walk starts at Bennett's Cross, about 2½ miles north-east of Postbridge on the B3212 Princetown to Moretonhampstead road. (Note: It is the second parking area after you pass the Warren House Inn if you are coming from the Postbridge direction.) You can recognise the place by the ancient cross alongside the road and the large information board in the parking area.

PARKING: There is a small parking area alongside the cross. If this is full, there is another ½ mile to the south-east, not far from the Warren House Inn.

MAPS: OS Outdoor Leisure 28 Dartmoor; OS Landranger 191 Okehampton and North Dartmoor (GR 680817; Grimspound 700808).

INTRODUCTION

Although it may seem a wild, sometimes inhospitable, place today, during the Bronze Age (about 2000–500 BC) Dartmoor's climate was somewhat milder, and there was a good living to be had here – as can be seen from the fact that across the moor the remains of about 4,000 huts from the period have been identified. This short walk enables you to experience the sense of freedom and space which are a hallmark of the open moors, and if you follow it in late summer you will have the added bonus of seeing the slopes covered in a purple carpet of heather. Apart from the main focus of the walk, the Bronze Age settlement of Grimspound, there is a wealth of other history to discover, from the ancient boundary marker of Bennett's Cross itself to extensive tin mining remains and a prehistoric stone row. There is some climbing involved, but the extensive moorland views make it worthwhile.

HISTORY

Many Bronze Age huts were isolated, others were grouped in small, loose settlements, and some, like those at Grimspound, were part of large communities within walled enclosures. The people led a mainly pastoral existence, herding animals, hunting deer and in some areas growing a few crops. It was a relatively peaceful time – the thick, high walls of the enclosure (probably about 10 ft high originally) were

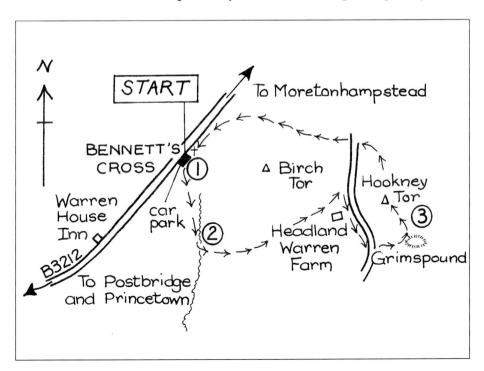

there for the protection of livestock rather than for any defensive purposes. The huts were circular, with walls about 4 ft high and from 5 to 8 ft thick, with banks of earth and large stones on the outside to improve insulation. They were roofed with heather, turf or rushes. The topsoil was removed from the inside to give a firm, flat floor which was a few inches below ground level. Some of the huts had sleeping platforms; in others the occupants slept on the floor. Likewise, some had screen walls at the entrances, which would have given added protection against the elements (since the entrances themselves would have been covered by no more than skins), while in others the doorways were unprotected.

It is believed that there was a major climate change between about 1000 and 500 BC which brought colder and bleaker conditions to Dartmoor. As a result people gradually abandoned the high ground, and by the time of the Iron Age only a few settlements on the fringes of the moor remained populated.

THE PLACE

Standing in the enclosure at Grimspound and looking out over the surrounding moorland, one can almost imagine what life was like for those early herdsmen. The landscape seems to have changed little – a road here, a farmhouse there, a few fields, but the rolling, heather-covered hills are timeless. The settlement itself has obviously fallen victim to the ravages of time, but the pattern is still clearly visible.

In addition to the enclosure, there are other features of historical interest to note along this route. Bennett's Cross is probably an ancient boundary marker, indicating the border of Headland Warren, where rabbits were 'farmed'; the letters 'WB' can be seen on the stone, indicating 'warren bounds'. Along the first part of the walk you will see extensive remains of the old tin workings and girts (long gulleys formed by the miners as they dug into the hillsides in search of the precious ore). The path also passes not far from a stone row, one of several on Dartmoor which probably predate even Grimspound, but whose precise significance is not clear.

THE WALK

❶ Facing away from the road, you will find three paths leading away from the parking area; take the right-hand one, which goes to the right of Birch Tor, roughly in the direction of a conifer plantation in the distance. You cross several tin workings and the path swings left

Bennett's Cross, near Postbridge

and descends to a valley. Follow it down the valley, through more workings and deep girts until you meet a track coming down from the right; bear left.

FOOD AND DRINK

The Warren House Inn is about ½ mile south-east of Bennett's Cross and despite its plain exterior, it is snug and welcoming inside. It retains its traditional atmosphere, with a bare floor and blackened beams, and it has a delicious range of homemade bar snacks, including sandwiches and ploughman's lunches, as well as main meals. Telephone: 01822 880208.

❷ You will come to a large grassy open area. Just beyond it there is a fork; go left. The path climbs along the side of Birch Tor beside a tin-miners' girt. As you approach the brow of the rise, you will see a stone row on the hillside to your right. As you go down the other side you will find a wall on your right; follow it to the path junction at the bottom of the hill. Go straight on (signposted to the road near Grimspound). When you get to the road, turn right. After about 700 yards you will come to a pull-in on the right, just before the road takes a right turn. Turn left here along a path which soon joins a small stream; follow it up the hill. The path crosses the stream and becomes paved, and after a short distance it emerges at Grimspound.

❸ From the enclosure, go to the north (left as you approach it), and follow the paved path up to Hookney Tor. Go over the tor and follow the path on the other side. Cross an old wall and turn left. Cross the road and continue along the clear path on the other side. This takes you round the other side of Birch Tor and brings you out at Bennett's Cross.

Walk 2
The Martyrdom of
St Hieritha – Chittlehampton
Length: 2¾ miles

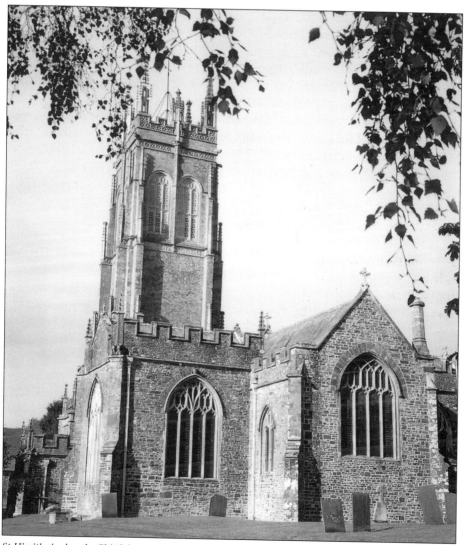

St Hieritha's church, Chittlehampton

HOW TO GET THERE: Turn south off the A361 Barnstaple to Tiverton road onto the B3226 just west of South Molton. On the outskirts of South Molton, turn right onto the B3227 and follow the signs for Chittlehampton.

PARKING: There is free parking in The Square, outside the church in the centre of the village.

MAPS: OS Explorer 127 South Molton and Chulmleigh; OS Landranger 180 Barnstaple and Ilfracombe (GR 635254).

INTRODUCTION

When pagan Saxons settled in an area lived in by Christian Celts, it was only a matter of time before conflict over religion claimed lives. Even in this quiet place, a young girl met a violent death for her faith. From the scene of Hieritha's martyrdom and her burial, farm paths and hedge-fringed lanes take you on a short, undemanding circuit of this delightful stretch of countryside. There are some pretty views, but the main attractions on this walk are the multitude of flowers to be seen along the way and the tranquillity – the silence broken only by the bleating of the sheep and the song of the birds.

HISTORY

Hieritha or Urith was born at East Stowford, just north of Chittlehampton, at the turn of the 7th and 8th centuries. She was a Christian Celt in an area recently settled by mainly pagan Saxons. When still a young woman, Hieritha was slain by a group of these Saxons, hacked to death with their scythes, apparently at the instigation of her pagan stepmother. The precise background to this horrific crime is not clear, but there was no doubt among subsequent generations that she died for her faith. Indeed, she was so revered during the Middle Ages that annual pilgrimages were made to Chittlehampton on her feast day (8th July), a practice that only ceased in 1539. The offerings made at her shrine by the medieval pilgrims were sufficient to pay for the erection of the magnificent tower which now stands at the west end of the church, over the chapel where she is believed to be buried. And so strong was her influence that Urith remained a very popular girl's name in families of all classes in the area for centuries after her death.

THE PLACE

The most likely location for the original St Urith's Well (the place where she is said to have died) is the pump in The Square, although it has also been suggested that the Bell Inn might have been built on

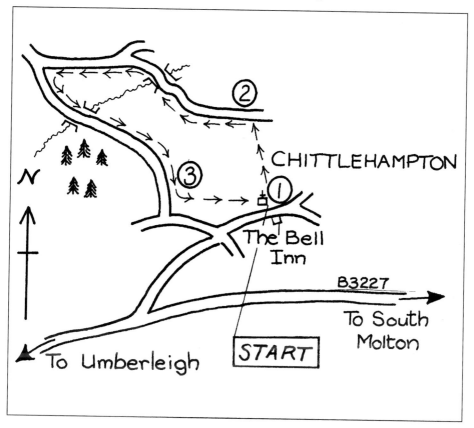

the site, or even that it was at the eastern end of the village. Her last resting place is more certain. She is believed to be buried under the small chapel to the north of the sanctuary (below the church tower), which became the focus of the medieval pilgrimages. It now leads to a vestry. There is also an effigy of her carved on the medieval pulpit, holding the palm of martyrdom and the foundation stone of the church. The church itself is a beautiful building which dates back to the 15th century; the tower is generally regarded as the finest in Devon.

THE WALK

❶ When you have visited the church, turn to the east (left as you leave the main door) and head for a gate at the far end of the churchyard; turn left up the track beyond. (Dogs are not allowed in the churchyard, so if you have one you should turn left from The

The village pump, believed to be on the site of St Urith's Well

Square and follow the road east for 100 yards or so before turning left up a small lane. This deteriorates into a track and you will soon see the gate from the churchyard on your left.) The track leads to a farm gate; go through and straight up a field to a stile. Go straight across the next field to another stile. Follow

the track on the other side to a third stile which leads into a lane.

❷ Turn left and follow the lane as it swings right, crosses a stream and then swings left. After about ¾ mile you come to a T-junction; turn left (signposted to Cobbaton and Barnstaple). After about 600 yards you will come to another T-junction; turn left again (signposted to Chittlehampton). This lane descends to a stream and then climbs through a wood.

❸ When it reaches the top of the rise it bends to the right. About

Chittlehampton

250 yards after it does so, turn left up the drive of a farm called Higher Biddacott, following the public footpath sign. (Do not turn left up the public bridleway on the bend itself.) Go through the farmyard and turn right along a track to a gate. Cross a field to another gate, and then bear slightly right across the next field to a third gate. Cross the cricket field on the other side towards a gap in the hedge on the far side. Just before you reach it, turn right down a track to yet another gate and follow the track beyond. This leads onto a lane which emerges onto The Square.

WALK 3
THE CITY THAT DEFIED THE CONQUEROR – EXETER'S CASTLE AND CITY WALLS

Length: 2½ miles

The Gatehouse, Rougemont Castle

HOW TO GET THERE: Exeter is at the junction of four main routes: the M5 from the north, the A38 from the south and the A30 from the east and west.

PARKING: There are several car parks around the city centre; the closest to the start of the walk is probably the multi-storey car park at the Guildhall Shopping Centre. However, the city can become very congested so you may prefer to make use of the park-and-ride scheme.

MAPS: OS Explorer 114 Exeter and the Exe Valley; OS Landranger 192 Exeter and Sidmouth, but a street map of Exeter (free from the Tourist Information Centre at the Civic Centre in Paris Street) is likely to be of more use (GR 921928).

INTRODUCTION

When the Normans arrived in England in 1066, Exeter was already over a thousand years old. Its city walls dated back to Roman times and had been considerably strengthened and repaired in the intervening centuries, providing a solid defence against any enemy – as William the Conqueror discovered early in 1068. This is a very easy stroll round Exeter's city walls, with a short detour along the River Exe. It takes in the remains of the Norman castle, the city's historic and delightfully restored quay area and several beautiful gardens.

HISTORY

The cause of Exeter's defiance of the new king is not clear, but it is known that William increased the ancient tribute which the city was required to pay the king, and also that Gytha, King Harold's mother, was in Exeter shortly after the conquest. It is likely, therefore, that both these factors contributed to the citizens' belligerent attitude. William demanded that the city swear allegiance to him, but it refused either to swear the oath or to pay the additional tribute – it would pay him the £18 per year required by ancient custom, but no more. William marched west in high dudgeon. The city fathers met him and gave him hostages against the city's good behaviour in future, but when they returned the citizens turned on them and repudiated their agreement.

William surrounded the city and attacked it daily, but the walls proved too strong, and although the people suffered, they continued to resist. William could not afford a long winter siege. Moreover, he realised that the longer Exeter held out, the more likely it was that rebellion would spread through the south-west – there were already reports of trouble in Cornwall. As a result, an agreement was reached after just eighteen days, according to which William swore not to

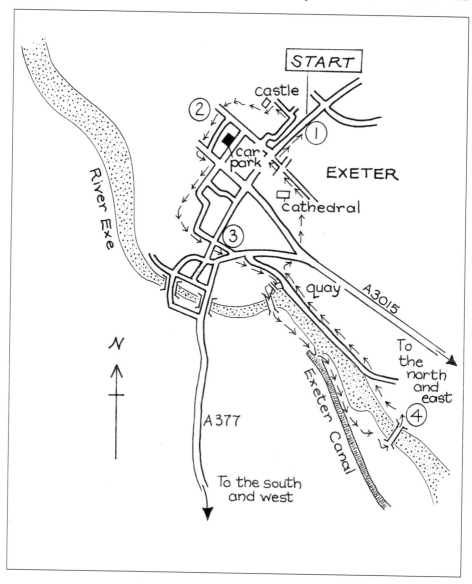

harm the city in any way, nor to increase the tribute required of it. Gytha was allowed to leave unharmed. Honour was therefore satisfied on both sides, but William was taking no more chances. A castle was immediately built on the mound known as Rougemont, in the north of the city, to ensure that no similar defiance could be offered in future.

THE PLACE

Although Exeter was heavily bombed during the Second World War, enough of the old city remains to provide a wealth of interest, and this is a walk through several different periods in the city's history. All that remains of the Norman castle is the gatehouse, but that is an imposing piece of architecture. Much of the old city wall remains, and despite the changes and the massive expansion of the urban area it is still possible to look out from it and imagine what it was like for the Saxon citizens manning the defences. The walk also passes some fine medieval architecture and visits the old quay, much of which dates back to Elizabethan times, and the Norman cathedral and its close.

THE WALK

❶ The walk starts in High Street, at the entrance to the Princesshay Shopping Centre, since that is close to where the park-and-ride buses stop. Cross the road and go along a cobbled passageway, following the pedestrian signs for the library and courts and Rougemont Castle and Gardens. Cross Musgrove Row into Castle Street and just before you come to the gate into the County Court, turn left through another gate. The red stone ruin on your right is the gatehouse of the original Norman castle. Follow the path immediately below the gatehouse as it goes round the mound. Where it forks, bear left alongside the city wall. Soon you will see a gap in the wall on your right, signposted to Northernhay Gardens; go through it and turn left to follow the outside of the wall to a gate.

❷ Go through and cross Queen Street into Northernhay Street. The line of the wall goes behind the buildings on your left, but most of it has been demolished along here. At the end of the street turn left and go up some steps. Turn right and cross the street to Bartholomew Street East, following the sign for the city wall walk. The wall is now on your right. When the street

> **FOOD AND DRINK**
>
> Exeter has a superb variety of pubs, tearooms and restaurants, including some delightful ones near the cathedral. But I prefer the ambience of the quay, and there are two I can recommend there, depending on whether your taste is for the traditional or the modern. The Prospect Inn is a 17th century establishment, full of atmosphere and character, and offers a range of traditional pub fare. Telephone: 01392 273152. Mango's, a few doors down, is a modern licensed restaurant offering sandwiches, filled baguettes and light lunches, including such delights as bacon and avocado on ciabatta. Telephone: 01392 438538. Both have tables outside overlooking the water.

Stepcote Hill

bends to the left, go straight on into a park. On the other side of the park the path passes in front of a terrace of houses and bends to the left. Follow it round and you will emerge on Bartholomew Street again. Go straight on to the junction.

❸ Cross New Bridge Street to West Street, following the pedestrian sign for Westgate. This takes you down past some lovely old houses and a church to Western Way. Bear right to cross the road and then go left; after a few yards, go down some steps (signposted to the city wall walk and the quay). At the junction halfway down the steps, turn left to follow the path that runs just below the wall. This emerges at the quay. Cross the road, pass the Riverside Cafe and turn right across a footbridge. Cross the next footbridge on your left and follow the quay round to the left alongside the water. Pass the Piazza Terracina and when you come to two locks turn left across one of them (signposted to the quay via the suspension bridge). At the path junction, go left (signposted to the quay via the suspension bridge again) and cross a footbridge over a floodplain. Go right and then left to cross the suspension bridge.

The Cathedral Close

❹ At the T-junction on the other side go left through a gate. Cross a drive and bear right along the river bank. You emerge, via another gate, onto the quay. At the end, bear right past the Customs House and then, where the road goes left, bear right again along a path to rejoin the city wall. Cross Western Way and then South Street to follow a path alongside the wall. At the junction go straight on and climb some steps to a street; turn left to enter the cathedral close. Pass the cathedral and at the end go straight on up a narrow lane (Martin's Lane) to High Street.

WALK 4
A MURDERER'S ATONEMENT? – SIR WILLIAM DE TRACEY AND MORTEHOE CHURCH

Length: 4 miles

The church of St Mary Magdalene, Mortehoe

HOW TO GET THERE: Turn west off the A361 Barnstaple to Ilfracombe road onto the B3343, which is signposted to Lee, Woolacombe and Mortehoe. After about 1½ miles, turn right, following the sign for Mortehoe.

PARKING: There is a pay-and-display car park on the left as you enter the village.

MAPS: OS Explorer 139 Bideford, Ilfracombe and Barnstaple; OS Landranger 180 Barnstaple and Ilfracombe (GR 457452).

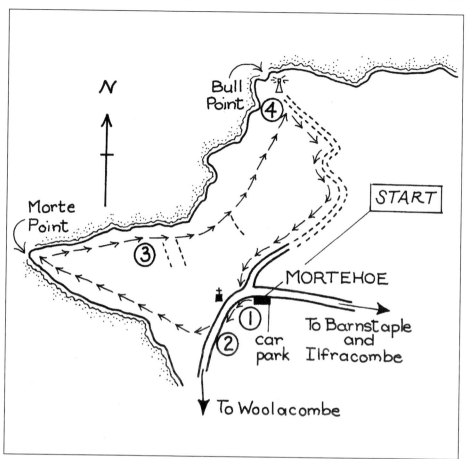

INTRODUCTION

Magnificent coastal views are the main feature of this walk, which follows the South West Coast Path for much of its route. They come at a price, however: there are some fairly stiff climbs to negotiate along the way. Having said that, there are several short cuts back to Mortehoe if you would like to shorten the route. There is also a chance to explore this pleasant village of slate-hung houses and to consider the question – did one of the murderers of St Thomas à Becket found the church here in an effort to atone for his dreadful crime?

HISTORY

'Will no one rid me of this turbulent priest?' Henry II's frustrated cry

as he found his plans to curb the power of the Church thwarted by
the Archbishop of Canterbury, Thomas à Becket, was taken all too
literally by four of his followers. On 29th December 1170 they burst
into Canterbury Cathedral and murdered Becket as he prayed. Henry
was appalled at the crime his unguarded words had instigated, and
the murderers scattered to avoid his wrath. One of them, Sir William
de Tracey, fled to North Devon and is said to have founded the
church of St Mary Magdalene at Mortehoe as atonement for his
involvement in the heinous deed.

He was at one time believed to have been buried there, and there
is certainly a tomb bearing an inscription to Sir William de Tracey to
be seen in the east transept of the church. However, it is now known
that he died in Calabria, and the tomb is in fact that of another
William de Tracey, who was Rector of Mortehoe and died in 1322.
The mystery surrounding the murderer deepens because, although
the de Traceys were a very well-known North Devon family (and a
frustratingly large number of them seem to have been christened
William), this particular man was not a member of that family at all
– at least not by birth. He assumed the surname upon his marriage to
Grace, the daughter of yet another Sir William de Tracey. So was the
church built by Becket's killer or by another bearer of that ubiquitous
name?

THE PLACE

St Mary's church was certainly founded at about the time de Tracey is
said to have fled to North Devon. It is in the centre of the old village,
set slightly above the rest of the buildings. It has an attractive lych
gate and a fine Norman doorway. Inside, it is an intriguing mixture
of the old and the comparatively modern. The pew ends are
interesting – they are carved with representations of various villagers.
And then, of course, there is the tomb in the east transept which was
once believed to hold our Sir William. Much of the inscription is now
illegible, but parts of it can still be deciphered.

THE WALK

❶ On leaving the car park, turn left to go into the village. Follow the
road round to the left; as you do so you will find the church on your
right. When you leave the church, turn right and continue along the
road out of Mortehoe and down a steep hill.

Rockham Bay and Bull Point

❷ About halfway down the hill you will see a gate on your right; go through it into a large field and follow the broad, grassy path down the hill. When it branches, take the left-hand fork to the bottom of the field and turn right to follow the Coast Path. Cross a stile and climb some steps to follow the path along the edge of a cliff for a short distance. It then runs through a broad grassy stretch before passing over the rocks round Morte Point. As you round the point you will see the lighthouse at Bull Point ahead of you.

❸ You climb quite steeply up to a headland and at the path junction go straight on, following the Coast Path. If you would like to cut your walk short at this point, turn right to return to Mortehoe. At the next junction go straight on again (or turn right for another short cut back to Mortehoe). The path

---

FOOD AND DRINK

Conveniently situated opposite the church is the Ship Aground, a delightful little inn which has been converted from three 16th century cottages. It offers a range of food, from pasties and burgers to fish, steak and vegetarian dishes, and an equally good selection of drinks. Telephone: 01271 870856.

climbs steeply round another headland, and then descends equally steeply on the other side.

Cross a stile and at the junction on the other side go straight on again (or take a final short cut by turning right). Another short climb follows, followed by another stile. Cross a field to yet another stile and another climb. The path swings right, away from the coast, for a short while. You climb another hill and the lighthouse comes into view again. Go down some steep steps and through a gate into another wide field.

❹ Just before you get to the lighthouse, turn right onto a surfaced track. Follow this away from the coast and you will come to a gate; go through it and follow the track as it turns sharply to the right and then to the left again. Ignore the two paths leading off to the left, signposted to Lee and Bennett's Mouth. The track eventually brings you to a second gate; follow the road on the other side back into Mortehoe. When you reach a T-junction, you will find the car park straight ahead of you.

WALK 5

'IN THE MORN THEY HANG AND DRAW, AND SIT IN JUDGEMENT AFTER' – LYDFORD CASTLE

Length: 3¼ miles

Lydford Castle, where the dungeon can still be seen

HOW TO GET THERE: Turn west off the A386 Okehampton to Tavistock road about 4 miles south of the junction with the A30, following the signs to Lydford.

PARKING: There is a free car park towards the end of the village, opposite the Castle Inn.

MAPS: OS Outdoor Leisure 28 Dartmoor; OS Landranger 191 Okehampton and North Dartmoor (GR 508847).

INTRODUCTION

Lydford Castle was built in 1195 as the seat of both the chief stannary court and the forest court, and as a prison to house

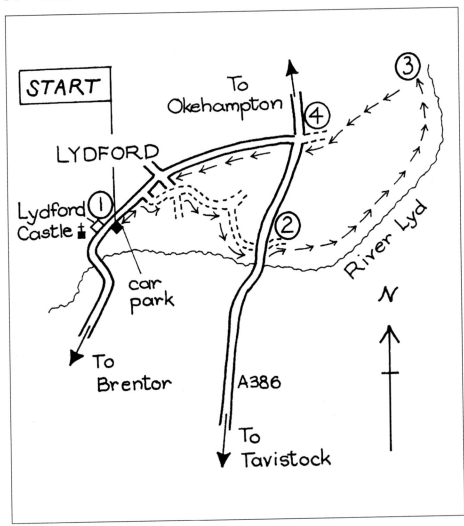

offenders found guilty in either. It, and the system of law that it supported, had a fearsome reputation and the town became notorious for 'Lydford Law'. After exploring the ancient town of Lydford, this route gives you a taste of the wild open spaces of Dartmoor without too much effort. There are some marvellous views, but the going can become rather wet in places after heavy rain, so appropriate footwear should be worn. The route described here can also be extended further out if you are feeling energetic and would like to experience the true grandeur of this undeveloped area of the moor. If you do venture further out, however, remember that this is part of a military range; if there are red flags flying from nearby tors, there is firing taking place and you should not proceed (the basic route does not cross the range).

HISTORY

It is not known when tin was first mined on Dartmoor, but the industry seems to have been well established by the 12th century. It was a small-scale affair, conducted by individuals or small groups, and provided a valuable source of income for the crown, since the duty paid went straight into the royal coffers. Because of their importance as mainstays of the king's wealth, the tinners were given an extraordinary degree of freedom: they paid no local or national taxes, and they had their own 'parliament' to regulate the industry, the Great Court, which met at Crockern Tor, near Two Bridges, as well as their own system of stannary courts. In time the influence of these courts was extended, so that at the height of their powers they could hear any case involving a tinner, whether it was a stannary matter or not. Since their juries consisted entirely of tinners, this meant that, in a dispute between a tinner and a non-tinner, the latter was unlikely to obtain justice. And anyone who opposed them or tried to curb their powers risked being accused (in the stannary courts, of course) of seeking to infringe their ancient rights and being imprisoned.

Dartmoor was also a royal forest or hunting ground, and as such subject to severe forest laws, which were aimed at preserving the game for the king's hunting pleasure. The locals were forbidden not only to kill any animals, but even to disturb or injure them or their cover. Offenders against both stannary and forest laws were sent to Lydford Castle, of which the 17th century Tavistock poet William Browne wrote:

> I oft have heard of Lydford Law,
> How in the morn they hang and draw,
> And sit in judgement after.

There is no evidence that men actually were hanged first and tried afterwards; it is more likely that this reputation originated in the system of courts used for trying cases under forest law. The actual trial was conducted by the Court of Swaincote, which met three times a year. If the offender was found guilty, the case was passed to the Court of Justice Seat for sentence to be passed. But since the latter met only once every three years, and since the sentence for certain offences was almost always death, the forest officials often decided that there was no point in having a condemned man taking up valuable prison space for three years and hanged the offender as soon as the verdict was announced, leaving the court simply to tidy up the paperwork.

THE PLACE

Now just a shell, Lydford Castle stands on a mound at the southern end of Lydford. The dungeon in which offenders were kept can still be seen, and even without its roof it is not hard to imagine what it must have been like in its heyday. It was no more than a 16-foot square pit, infested with rats, with no windows, and access only via a ladder. Indeed, in the 16th century it was described as 'one of the most annoious, contagious and detestable places within this realme' – which, given the state of prisons generally at that time, is quite a testimonial!

THE WALK

❶ Starting from the castle, turn left and walk through Lydford for about 300 yards until you come to Silver Street on your right. Turn into it, and continue along the track at the end. At the intersection, go straight on and follow the track as it passes under an old railway bridge. It then bends to the left and after 100 yards or so you will see another track going left; turn down that.

❷ It emerges onto the main road; cross to another track and go through a gate at the end onto the open moor. There are not many paths to follow here, but the going is easy. Keep to the high ground, with the River Lyd on your right. As the river curves left, follow it round, still keeping to the high ground.

❸ About a mile after passing through the gate onto the open moor, you will be faced by a

> **FOOD AND DRINK**
>
> The Castle Inn, alongside the castle, is a delightful hostelry, full of character and with an impressive menu, ranging from home-made steak and kidney pie to more exotic offerings such as Moroccan chicken. It also has an interesting display of Saxon coins minted in Lydford. Telephone: 01822 820241.

Lydford

wall. This is probably the best point from which to explore the moor further if that is what you want to do; simply turn right, cross a footbridge and, provided there are no red flags flying, walk as far as you like. To return to Lydford, however, turn left and follow the track alongside the wall.

❹ It comes out at a parking area; pass a gate and go down to another gate. Follow the track on the other side to the main road. Cross the road and follow the lane on the other side back into Lydford.

WALK 6
THE LORDS AND THE MERCHANTS – THE EXETER CANAL AND POWDERHAM CASTLE

Length: 7½ miles

Powderham Castle was built in 1390

HOW TO GET THERE: Turn east off the A379 Exeter to Dawlish road at Exminster and cross the railway line, following the signs to the Lions Rest Estate.

PARKING: There is an RSPB car park signposted to the right off this road just beyond the railway line. There is also parking at Powderham Castle.

MAPS: OS Explorer 110 (formerly 31) Torquay and Dawlish; OS Landranger 192 Exeter and Sidmouth (GR 953872; Powderham Castle 968835).

INTRODUCTION

The Exeter Canal was born out of conflict, following centuries of ill-feeling between the Earls of Devon, who built weirs across the River

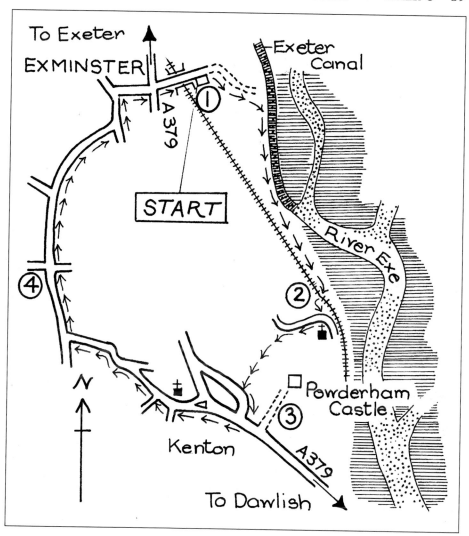

Exe, and the merchants of Exeter who saw their maritime trade cut off downriver. This gentle amble along the banks of the canal, famed for its birdlife, is followed by a walk across part of the Powderham estate to the village of Kenton and the castle itself. The return journey is along quiet country lanes filled with flowers in the summer, and with some good views along the way.

HISTORY

It all started with one Isabella de Fortibus, Countess of Devon, who in the 13th century built two weirs across the River Exe, presumably to feed water to various mills and industries she had established on her lands outside the city walls, in what is now called Countess Wear. The city fathers complained that the weirs interfered with their salmon fisheries, but to no avail, and there was at least a gap between them so that shipping could pass upriver to Exeter.

Far more serious – in fact disastrous – was the decision of Hugh Courtenay, who succeeded to Isabella's title and estates, to extend the weirs and build new ones in the 14th century. It appears that this was a deliberate manoeuvre to strangle the city's maritime trade and force all ships to discharge their cargoes (and pay the fees) at his own quay in Topsham. So ended a maritime tradition which stretched back to Roman times.

There followed two centuries of conflict. Exeter petitioned a succession of kings to force the Courtenays to demolish the weirs, but the latter were a significant power in the land, and the citizens received short shrift. Then in 1538 their luck changed. Henry Courtenay, Marquis of Exeter and head of the family, was accused of treason against Henry VIII. He was executed and his lands

The Exeter Canal, born out of conflict

confiscated. The city fathers seized their opportunity. In 1540 an Act of Parliament was passed allowing them to reopen the Exe to navigation. However, try as they might to remove the hated weirs, they proved immovable. They therefore built a canal to bypass them, and the city's maritime trade was resumed.

THE PLACE

The Exeter Canal stretches from the centre of the city to Turf, and for much of its length is a nature reserve. Today it is used mainly by pleasure craft.

The estate of Powderham came to the Courtenays from Margaret de Bohun, the granddaughter of Edward I, who married Hugh Courtenay, the 2nd Earl of Devon. On her death she bequeathed it to her fourth son, Sir Philip Courtenay, and it was he who built the castle, in 1390. It has been in the family ever since – although it was not used as their principal residence until after the execution of Henry, Marquis of Exeter – and the present Earl still lives there. It was fortified and held for the King during the Civil War, and like most similar stately homes has been extended and altered over the centuries. The castle and gardens are open from 10 am to 5.30 pm Sunday to Friday between April and October, and there are guided tours of the castle. There is also a farm shop and plant centre which is open all year round.

THE WALK

❶ Leave the car park and at the lane bear right. After about 600 yards it becomes an unsurfaced track and winds to the right and then to the left. It ends at a small car park; go through it and up some steps to the path alongside the canal. Turn right. After about ¾ mile you will pass the Turf Hotel on the other side of the water, and the locks that mark the end of the canal. The path goes to the right and through a kissing gate. On the other side it goes left through another gate and continues along the bank of the River Exe. After a little over ½ mile you go through another gate and then two more in quick succession to reach a railway line.

❷ Cross the line carefully, as it is used by high-speed trains. Go through another gate on the other side and turn left. You come out at a lane; turn right, passing a church as you go. When the lane swings to the right, go straight on across the broad grass verge, following the public footpath sign. Go through a kissing gate and follow the path along the left-hand side of the field beyond. Go through a gate at the end onto a path between fences. Cross a drive and go down some steps to a gate. Go through another gate and across a footbridge. On the other side, where the path forks, go left through a kissing gate, and through another gate at the end of the path into a lane. Turn left and follow the lane round to the right to join the main road; turn left and the entrance to Powderham Castle is about 200 yards down the road on the left.

> **FOOD AND DRINK**
>
> Perhaps the most pleasant place to be on a hot, sunny day is the Turf Hotel, which has a large garden overlooking both the River Exe and the Exeter Canal and serves a good range of food, but it is only open during the summer. Telephone: 01392 833128. There are two pubs in Kenton; my recommendation is the Devon Arms which has a good traditional pub menu, with steaks and sausages predominating, although there are, of course, vegetarian options. Telephone: 01626 890213. If you are looking for somewhere near the start of the walk, the Swan's Nest is a couple of hundred yards from the car park. Telephone: 01392 832371.

The Turf Hotel

❸ To continue the walk, turn right outside the castle entrance and retrace your route. Pass the lane you came up on and follow the main road into the centre of Kenton. Where it swings right, turn off left along Fore Street. At the end bear left along Church Street and at the junction go straight on. Follow the road round to the right, and at the junction just outside the village turn right along Chiverstone Road (signposted to Chiverstone Farm and Kenn). After about 700 yards you come to a T-junction; bear left and at the next junction go right.

❹ About ½ mile along this lane you will come to a crossroads; go straight on (signposted to Exminster). The lane climbs up a hill, with a wood on the right. At the next junction turn right (signposted to Exminster again). After a mile you come to another T-junction; turn left.

This lane takes you into Exminster. At the T-junction at the bottom of the hill turn right, and at the roundabout go straight on. At the next roundabout go straight on again and follow the lane on the other side past the Swan's Nest, following the sign to the Lions Rest Estate. Cross the railway line and the car park is on your right.

WALK 7
'A SHIPMAN OF DERT-E-MOUTHE' – JOHN HAWLEY AND DARTMOUTH CASTLE

Length: 4 miles

Dartmouth Castle

HOW TO GET THERE: There are three ways to get to Dartmouth: you can take the A3122, which runs east from the A381 Totnes to Kingsbridge road; you can follow the A379 from Paignton and catch the ferry across the River Dart at Kingswear; or you can take the A379 from Kingsbridge in the other direction.

PARKING: There is limited parking in the centre of Dartmouth, mainly along the North Embankment, and it tends to be quite expensive if you are staying any length of time. The car park for the park-and-ride scheme is on the edge of town along the A3122, and the charges are not unreasonable.

MAPS: OS Outdoor Leisure 20 South Devon; OS Landranger 202 Torbay and South Dartmoor (GR 878513; Dartmouth Castle 886502).

INTRODUCTION

In the late 14th century one man dominated Dartmouth – John Hawley, merchant, privateer, MP and, from Dartmouth Castle, defender against French invasion. This walk takes a slightly circuitous route to St Saviour's church, which has associations with Hawley, and then out of town, to enable you to explore Dartmouth's narrow streets and alleys that hide a multitude of architectural treasures. You then follow the line of the river to Dartmouth Castle before turning inland across rich, rolling farmland and returning to Dartmouth along a pretty, flower-filled, car-free lane. There is a steep climb initially, but the river and coastal views at the beginning and end of the walk are well worth the effort.

HISTORY

A Shipman was there dwelling far by Weste;
For aught I wot he was of Dert-e-mouthe.

So begins the description of one of the characters in Geoffrey Chaucer's *Canterbury Tales*, a character who is believed to have been based on John Hawley, owner of the *Magdelayne*, which is referred to in the *Tales*. Chaucer was an official of Edward III's government, and in 1373 he was sent to Dartmouth to investigate the seizure of a ship and cargo belonging to a merchant of Genoa. It was then that he would have met Hawley, who dominated the town between 1370 and his death – he was mayor fourteen times and member of parliament four times.

Hawley was a merchant, a shipowner and a privateer, licensed to attack and plunder enemy ships. For many Dartmouth seamen, however, there was a very fine line between privateering and piracy. The king valued their courage and skill, and did not even mind their ruthlessness towards their victims (such as throwing any captured sailors overboard), but he did not appreciate their occasional inability to distinguish between his friends and his foes – hence Chaucer's investigation into the incident with the Genoese vessel. Having said that, the king obviously trusted Hawley, because he became one of the senior commanders of the western fleet during the on-off Hundred Years' War with France. In 1388 he was asked to build a small fortress at the entrance to Dartmouth Harbour. Another fortress on the other side of the river enabled a chain to be drawn

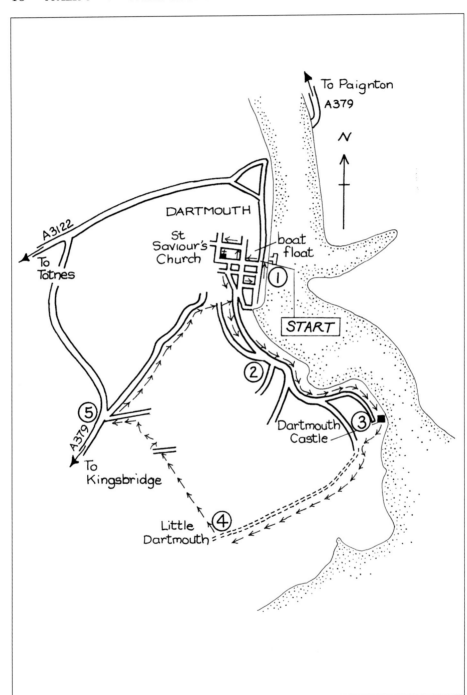

across to keep enemy ships out. Construction was halted in 1389 when a truce was signed with France, but was hastily resumed in 1403, when the truce broke down. In 1404 a Breton force landed at Slapton in an attempt to take Dartmouth from the rear. Hawley sent an army to meet them while remaining at Dartmouth Castle himself to defend the town against a possible sea attack. The Bretons were routed but by now Hawley was suffering from 'a severe disorder in one of my legs'. He died in 1408.

THE PLACE

In addition to a more general exploration of this lovely little town, the walk visits two locations particularly associated with John Hawley: St Saviour's church and Dartmouth Castle. The route also passes the site of his house, which became the Guildhall but was demolished in the 19th century. In St Saviour's church there is a memorial brass depicting Hawley and his two wives, Joanna and Alicia, on the floor of the chancel which he built. The church's rich furnishings bear witness to Dartmouth's prosperity at the time.

Dartmouth Castle is now maintained by English Heritage. Only one tower and part of the curtain wall of Hawley's original small fortress remain, but the castle was substantially extended and rebuilt in later years, and was put to use again as recently as the Second World War. It is open every day from April to October and every day except Monday and Tuesday from November to March. Opening times vary according to the time of year; telephone 01803 833588 for details.

THE WALK

❶ The route starts outside the Station Restaurant on the Embankment, between the small marina known as the Boat Float and the jetty from which the passenger ferry leaves. Turn inland alongside the Boat Float and at the top turn right into The Quay. After a short distance turn left up Duke Street, passing the museum on the right. Turn left again along Anzac Street to

FOOD AND DRINK

There is a tremendous choice of pubs, restaurants and tearooms in Dartmouth, with something to suit most tastes. My preference, however, is to take my refreshment along the way, at the Gunfield Hotel not far from the castle. It has a delightful terrace overlooking the river and offers a mouthwatering array of original seafood recipes, as well as meat and vegetarian dishes and a range of bar snacks. Telephone: 01803 834571.

St Saviour's church, Dartmouth

reach St Saviour's Square and the church. You will find the door round the corner on the south side. When you come out of the church, go down the street almost opposite the door. Cross Smith Street and follow Higher Street to its junction with Newcomen Road. On the left, where Lower Street, Higher Street and Newcomen Road meet, you will find a plaque commemorating the site where John Hawley's house stood. Turn right along Newcomen Street and follow it out of town.

❷ Where the road forks, go left, following the directions to the castle. After about 300 yards you come to another junction; turn left down Castle Road, following the sign for Dartmouth Castle. At the next fork, go left. When you come to the Gunfield Hotel, go left along a path, signposted to Dartmouth Castle.

❸ Beyond the castle, there is a choice of path; take the one that goes up the hill (signposted to Little Dartmouth). It climbs some steps and comes out onto a road; turn left, then immediately left again through a gateway. At the fork on the other side, take the unsurfaced path which is marked with the Coast Path acorn. At the next fork go right, again following the Coast Path acorn. You come out onto a surfaced track. After a few yards you come to another fork. Both directions are signposted to Little Dartmouth; take the right-hand one, which gives the distance as 1 mile. Follow the track to the Coastguard station and through a kissing gate into a field. Go through a gate at the end onto a track, which leads you to another gate and into a farmyard.

❹ At the track junction in the middle of the farmyard, turn right (signposted to Week Cottage). This track leads into a field. Keep to the right-hand side to reach a stile and follow the right-hand boundary of the next field as it bends to the left to go round a house. Go through a gate on the right onto a drive which after a few yards comes out at a lane; turn left. After about 50 yards, turn right up another drive (signposted to Swannaton). When the drive goes through a gateway, turn off left onto a rough track and at the fork go right as indicated by the yellow waymark. Follow the track past a house and round to the right. It brings you out onto another lane; turn left.

❺ After about 200 yards you come to a main road. Turn right and then, after a few yards, right again up a lane. After about 500 yards you will see a water tower on the left; just before you reach it the lane bends to the right and narrows. It then descends and you get a good view over the river ahead. About 600 yards after leaving the water tower the lane takes a sharp turn to the left; instead of following it, go straight on along a path (signposted to Ditcham Steps). It takes you down to a road on the edge of Dartmouth; turn left. When you come to Chapel Lane on the right, turn off and go down the steps. At the bottom turn left and at the fork go right along Newcomen Road. At the junction go straight across to Hauley Road and then left along the South Embankment to return to the Boat Float.

WALK 8
'A ROYAL COMPANION OF THE WORST SORT' – JOHN HOLAND OF DARTINGTON

Length: 4 miles

Dartington Hall

HOW TO GET THERE: The village of Dartington straddles the junction of the A384 and the A385 just northwest of Totnes. Dartington Hall can be approached from either road, in each case from just outside the village. The drive from the A385 is not signposted but is quite clear.

PARKING: There is a free car park opposite the entrance to the Hall.

MAPS: OS Explorer 110 (formerly 31) Torquay and Dawlish; OS Landranger 202 Torbay and South Dartmoor (GR 798627).

INTRODUCTION

John Holand was half-brother to Richard II, who granted him the manor of Dartington and made him Duke of Exeter. An eventful life ended in his execution. This exploration of the Dartington estate starts with a stroll through the beautiful Hall gardens. You can then visit the craft shops of the Cider Press Centre and finish with a delightful amble along the wooded banks of the River Dart, which are ablaze with wild flowers in summer. It is a lovely walk at any time, but the gardens are probably at their very best in spring and early summer.

HISTORY

John Holand was by all accounts not a nice man; the description in the title of this walk, by Bishop Stubbs, the 19th century constitutional historian, probably sums him up very well. He was intemperate, cruel, a bully and militarily inept. He and Richard were not close. Richard appears to have distrusted his character, certainly in his earlier years. A follower rather than a leader, Holand hitched his star to that of John of Gaunt, Duke of Lancaster, and married his daughter. He was granted the estate of Dartington, among others, in 1384, but his tenure did not last long. In 1385 some of his followers became involved in a fight with those of the Earl of Stafford and one was killed. Rather than let the law take its course, Holand picked a fight with Stafford's son and killed him. He was summoned for murder and all his possessions, including Dartington, were confiscated. John of Gaunt interceded on his behalf, however, and he was pardoned.

He and Gaunt diplomatically withdrew from England to pursue the latter's claim to the Castilian throne – a disastrous campaign in which Holand signally failed to prove himself as a military leader. On their return Richard, desperately short of supporters, made Holand Earl of Huntingdon and granted him various estates, including Dartington again. From then on, Holand became a staunch supporter of the king. He was made Admiral of the Fleet west of the Thames (a post in which he failed to distinguish himself) and, in 1397, after helping to put down a rebellion, during which he was said to have been implicated in the murder of the Duke of Gloucester and the Earl of Arundel, he was created Duke of Exeter.

He did not enjoy his new status for long. In 1399, soon after the death of Holand's patron Gaunt, the latter's son, Henry Bolingbroke,

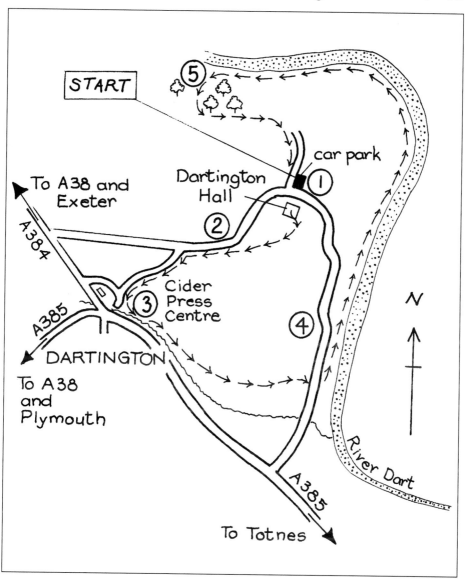

returned from exile to lead a rebellion against the king. Richard was defeated and forced to abdicate, and Bolingbroke assumed the throne as Henry IV. Richard's few remaining supporters, including Holand, were stripped of all titles and holdings granted since 1397, which meant that Holand lost the dukedom of Exeter. To his credit, Holand's loyalty did not waver. He continued to support Richard as

The Tiltyard, Dartington Hall

the true king and led a rebellion against Henry. However, he overestimated both Richard's support in the country and his own military abilities. The uprising failed and Holand was executed by the families of the two men he was said to have murdered in 1397.

THE PLACE

Dartington Hall is without doubt one of the most impressive examples of medieval English domestic architecture still surviving. The main buildings were erected between 1390 and 1399 and form a rectangle surrounding a beautiful courtyard. The focal point is Holand's Great Hall, opposite the massive entrance gate. There are lodgings and offices along the two sides and a large barn, now a theatre, next to the gate.

By the 1920s, the place had fallen into some disrepair and was bought by a couple of wealthy philanthropists, Leonard and Dorothy Elmhirst, who restored it as the centre of a wide-ranging enterprise to promote their two great passions of rural regeneration and educational innovation. It was they who laid out the magnificent gardens, into which they incorporated the tiltyard which was used by Holand for his jousting tournaments. The enterprise is now administered by a trust. The courtyard and gardens are open to the public all year round; they are beautiful at any time, but especially so in spring and early summer. The buildings, however, now form part of an art college and conference centre; the only part to which there is public access is the Great Hall, and then only when it is not in use. It is a magnificent building, and round the walls you will see banners depicting the various activities in which the Dartington Hall Trust has been involved. There are also the badges of the estate's various owners. There is no entrance fee, but there is a box at the gate for voluntary donations to the gardens' upkeep.

THE WALK

❶ Cross the road from the car park to the enormous wooden gate which leads into the courtyard. (Note that dogs are not allowed into the gardens so, if you have one, you should turn right at the road and follow it round to rejoin the route where it emerges from the gardens at point 2 below.) To reach the gardens, go to the left of the Great Hall. Follow the path round, keeping the Great Hall on your right, and you will come to the Tiltyard. This is the heart of the gardens, and they can be explored via a variety of different paths. When you have had your fill, aim for the far right-hand corner of the gardens as you look out across the Tiltyard from in front of the Great Hall. There you will find a gate; go out onto a road and turn left.

❷ Follow the footpath alongside the road for a short distance and at the junction, turn left (signposted to the Foxhole Centre and the White House Conference Centre). You pass a couple of entrances on your left and go through a gate. Pass a car park on your right and go through another gateway into a lane.

❸ Go straight on to reach the main part of the Cider Press Centre, with its craft and other shops, or bear left to continue

> **FOOD AND DRINK**
>
> The White Hart bar, alongside the Great Hall in the courtyard of Dartington Hall itself, has organic wine and local real ales on offer, as well as a mouthwatering array of food, ranging from baguettes to such delicacies as squash and parmesan risotto and peppered venison. Telephone: 01803 847111.
> Alternatively, Cranks Restaurant at the Cider Press Centre offers coffees, teas and delicious wholefood light lunches when the Cider Press Centre itself is open (from Monday to Saturday, and on Sundays from Easter to Christmas). Telephone: 01803 862388.

the walk. At the junction follow the main lane round to the right. When you come to a shop called Bazaar, turn left and pass to the right of Tridias. You are now on a path alongside a little stream. Where it forks, go left slightly away from the stream, and at the next fork go straight on. The path then rejoins the stream; go straight on, following what is now a broad path alongside the water. At the next fork go left. You pass a flood plain on your right and cross two cattle grids. Eventually you pass through a gateway onto the drive up to Dartington Hall; turn left. Follow the drive for about 300 yards or so and you will see a stile alongside a gate on your right.

❹ Cross it into a field and follow the path on the other side alongside the River Dart. It is a long field, and at the end you cross a stile and enter a small copse. You emerge into an area covered in bracken and Himalayan balsam and cross another stile into another long field. You pass a concrete track and at the end of the field enter a small copse. Go through a gap in a wall and leave the copse to cross yet another long field. At the end you cross a stile into a small wood.

❺ Here you are faced with three paths: one sharp left up the side of the wood, one straight on along the bottom edge and one half left, between the two. Take the middle one, a clear track which climbs gently up a hill and then curves left alongside a wall to climb more steeply. When it goes through a gate turn off it onto a narrower path. This eventually brings you to a stone stile into a field; turn left and after a short distance cross a wooden stile onto a track. At the end cross another stile onto a road; turn right and after about 400 yards you will find the car park on your left.

WALK 9
'A VALIANT MAN AND TRUE' – BIDEFORD'S MOST FAMOUS SON

Length: 5 miles

Bideford's attractive parish church

HOW TO GET THERE: Bideford is at the junction of two major roads: the A386 and the A39. The walk starts at The Quay, in the centre of the town.

PARKING: There is a car park at the northern end of The Quay.

MAPS: OS Explorer 139 Bideford, Ilfracombe and Barnstaple; OS Landranger 180 Barnstaple and Ilfracombe (GR 455269).

INTRODUCTION

Bideford's history is closely bound up with that of the Grenville family – indeed, until the 18th century, the town actually belonged to them. It was a quiet backwater for much of its existence, although it did become a borough in the 13th century. It rose to prominence, however, during the reign of Queen Elizabeth, largely owing to the efforts of its most famous son, Sir Richard Grenville. Combining town and country walking, riverside trails and woodland paths, flower-filled hedgerows and superb views, this route has variety and interest in abundance. It takes you along Bideford's historic quay to visit the parish church, with its reminders of Sir Richard Grenville, then crosses the 15th century Bideford Bridge to join the Tarka Trail, a long-distance path which explores the area in which Henry Williamson's classic *Tarka the Otter* is set, and which follows a disused railway line beside the River Torridge along this stretch. You return to Bideford via lanes and woodland tracks and paths, with grand views over the rolling farmland and the Torridge estuary. There are a couple of stiff climbs in the middle of the walk, but otherwise the going is very easy.

HISTORY

Born in 1542, Sir Richard was the son of Roger Grenville, the commander of Henry VIII's ill-fated vessel, the *Mary Rose*, who died when the ship sank off Portsmouth on its way to attack the French. Although he was destined to become one of several Devon seafarers who dominated maritime affairs in Elizabethan times – a select band which also included his cousin, Sir Walter Raleigh, Sir Francis Drake and Sir Humphrey Gilbert – Richard's early adult years were spent soldiering, first in Hungary and then in Ireland.

He soon became interested in the sea, however, though it was not until 1585 that he succeeded in getting a major venture off the ground. In that year he commanded a fleet to colonise the American territories of Virginia and Carolina, and established a flourishing trade in tobacco and other products between them and Bideford, a trade that was to last until the independence of the American colonies 200 years later. He also brought back from the colonies an Indian servant, whom he named Raleigh after his cousin – the first Native American to set foot on British soil. Sadly, he survived only a year.

In 1588, Grenville joined Drake's fleet in battle with the Spanish Armada, and in 1591 he was second-in-command to Lord Thomas Howard on a voyage to the Azores with the aim of waylaying the Spanish treasure ships. His vessel, the *Revenge*, was cut off from the rest of the fleet but, rather than flee the approaching Spaniards, he decided to stay and fight – one ship and 190 men against 15 Spanish vessels manned by 5,000 men. Fifteen hours later, after inflicting

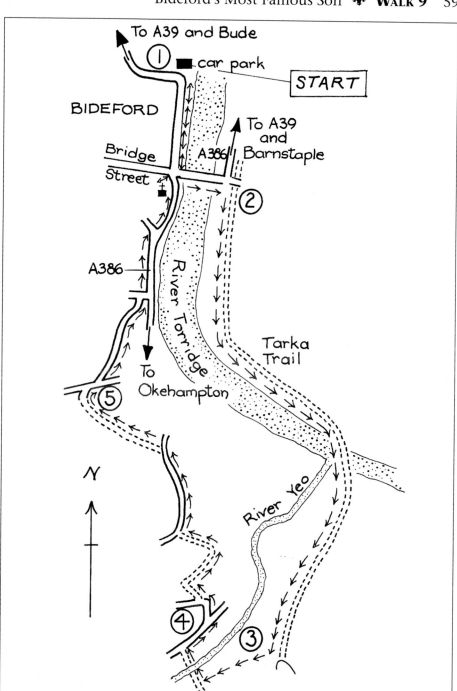

To A39 and Bude

① ■ car park

START

BIDEFORD

To A39
and
Barnstaple

Bridge
Street

A386

A386

②

River Torridge

Tarka
Trail

To
Okehampton

⑤

N

River Yeo

④

③

heavy losses on the enemy, he was wounded and surrendered. He died a few days later. His final words are said to have been:

> I have fought for Queen and Faith like a valiant man and true;
> I have only done my duty as a man is bound to do:
> With joyful spirit I Sir Richard Grenville die.

Valiant and true he undoubtedly was, but historians believe that his death and that of so many of his men was caused not by his doing his duty 'as a man is bound to do', but by the violent temper for which he was renowned and which prevented him from assessing the situation clearly and logically.

THE PLACE

Bideford's quay dates back to the 17th century, when the American trade established by Grenville was at its height. The parish church, just off Bridge Street, is a mainly 19th century structure, but the tower was part of the original building erected by one of Sir Richard's ancestors in the 13th century. It is a most attractive church, with

Bideford bridge

some lovely stained glass. On the right of the Lady Chapel, to the right of the altar, is a brass tablet which records Sir Richard's death and his epitaph, and in the porch are photographs of the baptismal and burial certificates of his servant Raleigh. There is a 20th century memorial to him in the form of a large sheet of glass near the entrance, which depicts Sir Richard with a Devon fisherman, the Virgin Mary, Mother Theresa and St Boniface of Crediton – an interesting collection of characters! On the corner of Bridge Street and New Road, just opposite the bridge, is the Town Hall, another 19th century building, which stands on the site of the Grenvilles' town house.

THE WALK

❶ Walk along The Quay until you come to the bridge. Turn right just opposite it, into Bridge Street, and then take the first left into Church Walk to reach the church. Return to the bridge, passing the Town Hall, and cross the River Torridge. At the mini-roundabout on the other side go straight on, but almost immediately beyond it climb some steps on the right to reach the Tarka Trail at the old Bideford Station.

❷ Turn right and pass the station buildings. The Trail follows a disused railway track past some saltmarshes alongside the river. About a mile after joining it, you cross the river and follow the valley of the River Yeo, a tributary of the Torridge.

❸ Just over ½ mile after crossing the river, look out for a path going off the Tarka Trail to the right, just before the Trail enters a tunnel. There is a signpost pointing to Landcross, but it is a few yards along the path, and is therefore not obvious. (If you find yourself at the tunnel, you have gone too far.) Take the path up a short hill and at the top turn right across a stile. Follow the posts which indicate the path across the field beyond,

FOOD AND DRINK

There are any number of watering holes in Bideford, as well as restaurants and cafes. A very pleasant old pub, with a lot of atmosphere, right next to the church and therefore directly on our route is the Tavern in the Port, on the corner of Bridge Street and Church Walk. It offers an interesting variety of jacket potatoes, filled baguettes and what they call 'nibbles' as well as more substantial fare such as lasagne and Cajun marinated chicken. Telephone: 01237 423334.

bearing half-left to another stile. You enter a little wood and after a short while cross another stile into a field. At the end, yet another stile takes you onto a track; turn right. Cross a bridge and when you come to a road turn right.

❹ After about 150 yards, turn left up a lane; where this takes a sharp turn to the left, go straight on up a green lane marked 'Unsuitable for motor vehicles'. The track twists and turns between stands of trees, climbing steadily as it goes, and after some 500 yards it emerges onto another lane; turn right. The lane descends gently and bends to the left. When it swings right again, opposite the entrance to Ashridge Barton, go straight on down another green lane. This leads you through a wood to a lane; go straight on.

❺ Follow the lane round to the right, and at the junction go straight across to climb into another wood. You emerge at the top of a hill and pass some houses on your right. The lane then descends quite steeply to a junction; turn right and then immediately left onto the main road on the outskirts of Bideford. At the next junction, go straight on into the centre of town, past the bridge and along The Quay to the car park.

WALK 10
THE MOST FAMOUS PRIVATE CITIZEN IN THE WORLD – SIR FRANCIS DRAKE AT BUCKLAND ABBEY

Length: 4½ miles

Buckland Abbey, home of the Drake family

HOW TO GET THERE: The village of Buckland Monachorum is 2 miles west of the A386 Plymouth to Tavistock road.

PARKING: There is a church car park on the left as you enter the village, which the public are allowed to use when there are no services in progress. Otherwise there is limited parking in the road.

MAPS: OS Outdoor Leisure 28 Dartmoor; OS Landranger 201 Plymouth and Launceston (GR 489682; Buckland Abbey 487665).

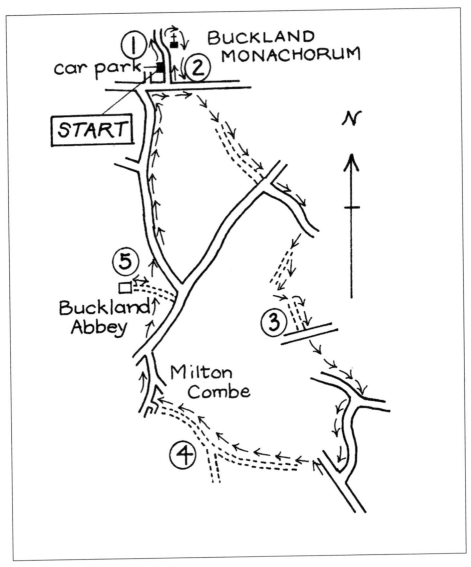

INTRODUCTION

Sic Parvis Magna – 'Great things from small beginnings' – was the motto Sir Francis Drake chose for his coat of arms, and a more apt slogan would be hard to find. He came from humble yeoman stock and was one of eleven children, yet he rose to become the most famous private citizen in the world. This is a relatively easy ramble across farm fields and down quiet lanes and tracks in the countryside

Drake knew well. It takes in the picturesque villages of Buckland Monachorum (with a chance to see Drake's own pew in the church) and Milton Combe, as well as Drake's home at Buckland Abbey, and there are some good views.

HISTORY

Born not far from Buckland in about 1540, Francis Drake spent much of his childhood in Kent, but always regarded Devon as his home. His first transatlantic voyage was carrying slaves to the Caribbean in 1568, but his main claim to fame was as the scourge of the Spanish. Three times in the early 1570s he raided the Spanish Main, attacking treasure fleets and making himself a very rich man in the process.

Perhaps his most outstanding feat was his circumnavigation of the globe between 1577 and 1580, from which he again managed to return laden with Spanish booty – enough, it was said, to fund the government for a whole year. Queen Elizabeth knighted him in recognition of his achievement, and with some of the proceeds of his journey he bought Buckland Abbey from his fellow-mariner, Sir Richard Grenville.

He played a prominent part in local affairs, serving as Mayor of Plymouth in 1581. He was a driving force in the city's development, building up its trade and bringing in a water supply from the headwaters of the River Meavy via a leat which still bears his name.

However, he was still happiest at sea, especially when making life difficult for his Spanish foes. He undertook more raids on the Spanish Main in the mid-1580s, and was prominent in fighting off the Armada in 1588 – the story of his refusal to interrupt his game of bowls on Plymouth Hoe, although probably apocryphal, has become the stuff of legends. What is beyond doubt, however, is that as Vice-Admiral of the fleet he played a major part in the victory, harrying the Spaniards in the Channel and finally driving what remained of the Armada off into the North Sea.

He saw his beloved Devon for the last time in 1595, when he set off for the Caribbean once more. He died on board his ship on 28th January 1596. Despite two marriages he had no children to inherit his estates, and Buckland Abbey passed to his younger brother Thomas.

THE PLACE

Buckland Abbey was founded as a Cistercian house in 1278. After the

Picturesque Milton Combe

Dissolution of the Monasteries in 1539, Henry VIII sold it to Sir Richard Grenville, a landowner from North Devon. It eventually passed to his grandson, also Sir Richard, a seafaring contemporary of Drake's, from whom the latter bought it in 1580. It remained in the Drake family until the middle of the 20th century, and is now owned by the National Trust. It is not a particularly large house, but it has some very interesting outhouses and craft workshops, and the main building houses some fascinating displays of Drake relics. It is open from 10.30 am to 5.30 pm every day except Thursday between April and October and from 2 pm to 5 pm at weekends from November to March.

The church of St Andrew in Buckland Monachorum is also worth a visit. Set against the north-west wall, behind the font, is Drake's original pew, decorated with a carving of the *Golden Hind* on a globe, and to the south of the chancel is the Drake Chapel, which commemorates subsequent generations of the family.

THE WALK

❶ Turn left from the car park and walk into the centre of the village.

The church is on your right. Our route follows a path round to the right beyond it, which can also be reached from the churchyard. It passes through a kissing gate and crosses a stone stile. At the path junction just beyond the stile, turn right. After a while you go through another kissing gate and cross a footbridge on your right. At the junction on the other side, go straight on along

> **FOOD AND DRINK**
>
> My recommendation for good food in delightful surroundings is the Drake Manor Inn in Buckland Monachorum. It is full of character and offers an interesting and varied array of fish, meat and vegetarian dishes. Telephone: 01822 853892. If you would prefer to stop along the way, try the Who'd Have Thought It in Milton Combe. Telephone: 01822 853313

the right-hand side of the field. Go through a gap in a line of trees and continue to follow the right-hand boundary until you emerge onto a lane.

❷ Turn left and after about 50 yards turn right across a stile into a field, following the footpath sign. Keep to the right of the field and when you come to some bushes go straight on through them. You will come to a stile on your left; cross it and go half-left across the field to another stile. Go straight on along the track on the other side. It takes you through two gates; continue to follow the track along the edge of two fields until you emerge through a gate onto a lane. Cross it to another lane (signposted to Venton and Stokehill). After about 500 yards the lane takes a sharp turn to the left; go straight on through a gate, following the public footpath sign. Bear right across a field. About halfway across you will come to a track; bear left and follow it to a gate. Follow the track along the left-hand side of the next field to another gate and turn left immediately beyond it. When you get to the end of the field, follow the boundary round to the right to a small gate. Keep to the left of the next field to reach a gate onto a lane.

❸ Cross the lane to a gate and cross the field on the other side to another gate. Keep to the left of the next field to yet another gate leading onto a track. Turn off right and go down to cross a stream and then go through a kissing gate to a lane. Turn left. (Note: At the time of writing, the County Council is considering a diversion of the public right of way, and the route just described follows that diversion. If the diversion is rejected, however, then the route will

St Andrew's church, Buckland Monachorum

continue along the track, go through a farmyard and emerge onto the lane a little higher up. Either way, the path should be clearly marked.)

Follow the lane up a hill and at the T-junction go right. You cross a cattle grid onto a short stretch of moorland and come to another T-junction. Turn right and almost immediately left across a stile into a field. Keep to the left and at the end cross a stile onto a track. Follow the track through more gates with stiles alongside, and where it turns left into a field carry straight on along a broad, grassy path.

❹ At the end cross a stile onto a much clearer track; turn right. At the junction bear slightly left and you will come out onto a lane. Bear right and follow the lane down to the village of Milton Combe. At the bottom turn right and at the next junction go left and climb a hill out of the village. At the junction at the top of the hill, go straight across to a stile. Follow the path on the other side to a bus circle and then cross another stile into a field. Go through a gate, cross a track and go through another gate. At the end of the next field go through yet another gate, cross a drive and go along a track. At the next drive go left to visit Buckland Abbey.

❺ When you reach the track on your way back from the abbey, go past it and turn immediately left through a kissing gate into a field, following the yellow waymark. Keep to the left to reach a kissing gate leading into a wood. After a short distance you will come to another kissing gate; go through and cross a lane to yet another kissing gate. Follow the path up through the wood to the last kissing gate, which takes you onto a road; turn left. After about 600 yards you will come to a junction; go straight on (signposted to Buckland Monachorum). After another 600 yards there is a T-junction; turn right (signposted to Buckland Monachorum and Crapstone), and take the second turning on the left to return to the village.

THE LAST MAJOR BATTLE OF THE CIVIL WAR – GREAT TORRINGTON

Length: 2½ miles

The Black Horse Inn

HOW TO GET THERE: Great Torrington is on the A386 between Okehampton and Bideford.

PARKING: The walk starts at the Castle Hill car park in the town centre. There are two car parks signposted from the main road; follow the signs for the one with 280 spaces, not the smaller, 70-space one.

MAPS: OS Explorer 126 Clovelly and Hartland; OS Landranger 180 Barnstaple and Ilfracombe (GR 495190).

INTRODUCTION

This short and easy walk starts at the Torrington 1646 Heritage Centre, which focuses on the town's part in the English Civil War. It

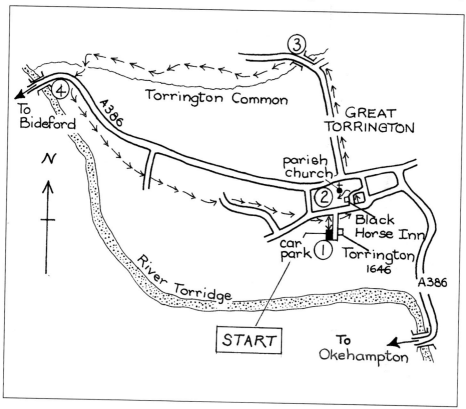

then visits a couple of the main sites of the last major battle of the war, which raged through Torrington's streets, before heading for the beautiful open spaces of Torrington Common, part wood, part heathland. After a circuit of the Common, with some lovely views, we return, via quiet streets, to Castle Hill.

HISTORY

Torrington was the scene of two skirmishes early in the Civil War, and of the last major battle towards the end of the conflict. In 1642 the Royalists occupied the town with a view to using it as a springboard from which to attack the Parliamentary forces in North Devon. However, the Parliamentarians got in first and took the town from them. By 1643 the Royalist troops were again in occupation and Cromwell's men again tried to take it, this time without success.

The town remained in Royalist hands until a cold, dark night in February 1646, when two large armies, totalling about 15,000 men, met and fought their way through its streets and over the Royalist barricades. Lord Hopton commanded the Royalist Army of the West while the Parliamentarian New Model Army was led by Sir Thomas Fairfax and Oliver Cromwell.

During the battle, Fairfax imprisoned 200 Royalist soldiers in the parish church, unaware that Hopton had been using it to store his gunpowder. In the middle of the conflict 80 barrels of powder exploded, killing all the prisoners and their guards. At first it was believed that the explosion was an accident, but Robert Watt, one of Hopton's soldiers, was found among the rubble and was accused of being responsible. It was said that Hopton had paid him to destroy the cache, presumably to prevent it from falling into the Parliamentarians' hands.

THE PLACE

Castle Hill, where the walk begins, was where the Prince of Wales's Regiment of Foot, the last Royalist troops to leave Torrington, were stationed. They escaped down the steep hill at the end of the car park. It is now also the site of the Torrington 1646 Heritage Centre, which gives an insight into 17th century life and explains what happened during the Battle of Torrington. It is open Tuesday to Saturday (all week during school holidays) between 10.30 am and 5 pm from April to September and between 11 am and 4 pm from October to March.

The Black Horse Inn in High Street, which you pass along the route, is believed to be where Lord Hopton had his headquarters. The walk also visits the parish church, the scene of the devastating explosion on the night of the battle. It was substantially damaged, but was rebuilt in 1651. A stone in the wall of the transept just to the right of the main door records the event and the rebuilding. The mound to the south of the church is believed to be the burial site of the soldiers killed in the explosion.

THE WALK

❶ Leave the car park and turn right. Take the first turning on the left, which is High Street, and you will see the Black Horse Inn on the left. At the end of the street, where it turns to the right, go straight on down an alley to the churchyard.

❷ After visiting the church, aim for the gate about halfway along the

St Michael's church, Great Torrington

churchyard on the far side and cross the main road to School Lane, following the signs to Weare Giffard and Dartington Crystal. This takes you out of town and down into a valley. It swings to the left and crosses a small bridge.

❸ A short distance beyond the bridge you will see a public footpath sign pointing half-left into a wooded area. Follow it and you will see a stone indicating that the path you are on is called the Barmaid's Path. Where it forks bear right and follow the main path above a stream. After about 750 yards the Barmaid's Path crosses a broad track. Continue to follow it on the other side, and at the next fork follow the main, surfaced path to the left. It leads you to a footbridge across the stream, and on the other side you will see a stone indicating that you are now on Centenary Path. Go through a barrier and at the junction just beyond it turn right. After a short distance, you emerge onto the A386.

❹ Cross carefully, as it is a busy road, and follow the surfaced path on the other side. It takes you high above the River Torridge and after about 600 yards comes out at a road. Cross over and at the fork take the left-hand path (signposted to Great Torrington). The path joins a lane; carry straight on and when the lane joins a more major road carry straight on again. When the road swings right down a hill go straight on along a path, following a pedestrian sign for Great Torrington. After about 100 yards you emerge onto another road, and after a few more yards there is a junction. Go straight on and after another 100 yards or so you will see the entrance to the car park on your right.

> **FOOD AND DRINK**
>
> Torrington is well served with pubs and restaurants, but where else would one take refreshment on this walk than at the Black Horse Inn? I can warmly recommend this pub, not only for its historical associations but also for its character and atmosphere, and for its mouthwatering menu, which ranges from bar snacks to daily specials such as honey roast chicken and local pork. Telephone: 01805 622121.

WALK 12
'FATHERS AND MOTHERS IN A STRANGE LAND' – THE HUGUENOT REFUGEES OF BARNSTAPLE

Length: 2¼ miles

Queen Anne's Walk, Barnstaple

HOW TO GET THERE:
Barnstaple is at the junction of three major roads: the A361, the A377 and the A39. The walk starts in the town centre.

PARKING: The most convenient car park is the one at Queen Street, which is signposted as you approach the town centre.

MAPS: OS Explorer 139 Bideford, Ilfracombe and Barnstaple or Outdoor Leisure 9 Exmoor; OS Landranger 180 Barnstaple and Ilfracombe (GR 560332).

INTRODUCTION

The Huguenots were Protestants who had long been in conflict with the French authorities. In 1685 their right to freedom of conscience was revoked and many were forcibly converted to Catholicism, while others were killed or sent to the galleys. Some 400,000 of them fled abroad to escape this persecution, and many came to Barnstaple. Here a fascinating stroll through the medieval heart of Barnstaple to the River Taw, once busy with shipping, is followed by a pretty amble along the riverbank and back along the other side. It takes in the 14th century St Anne's Chapel, the parish church (which dates back to the 12th century), some beautiful 17th century almshouses, the Barnstaple Heritage Centre, the 15th century Long Bridge across the Taw and the Barnstaple and North Devon Museum.

HISTORY

Barnstaple has a long history, stretching back to pre-Norman times, but it really flourished in the 17th and 18th centuries, when it was a major centre of trade (and of privateering – the licensed raiding of enemy shipping). This was also the time when it played host to Huguenot refugees from France. One of these was Jacques Fontaine, who managed to slip aboard the trading vessel *Industry* at La Rochelle with a small party of fellow refugees, including his sister and his fiancée, Elizabeth-Anne Boursiquot. They came ashore on Sunday, 1st December and were immediately taken to their hearts by the citizens of the town. Jacques found shelter with a rich merchant, Joseph Downe, and his sister, while his fiancée was taken in by the Fraine family.

Jacques settled in well with the Downes – almost too well, it seems, for according to his memoirs Miss Downe grew overly attached to him and finally even suggested marriage, dangling her fortune before him as an incentive. He remained true to his original love, however, and he and Elizabeth-Anne were married in the parish church in February 1686. The locals were generous with their gifts and the young couple were soon made comfortable in their own home. They eventually moved to Taunton and had six children. But they never forgot their friends in Barnstaple. Jacques wrote in his memoirs: 'The good people of Barnstaple were full of compassion, they took us into their houses and treated us with the greatest kindness. Thus God raised up for us fathers and mothers in a strange land.'

But why did they, and many more of their compatriots, choose Barnstaple? One reason may have been that several merchants in the town had trading links with Huguenot businesses in France, and at

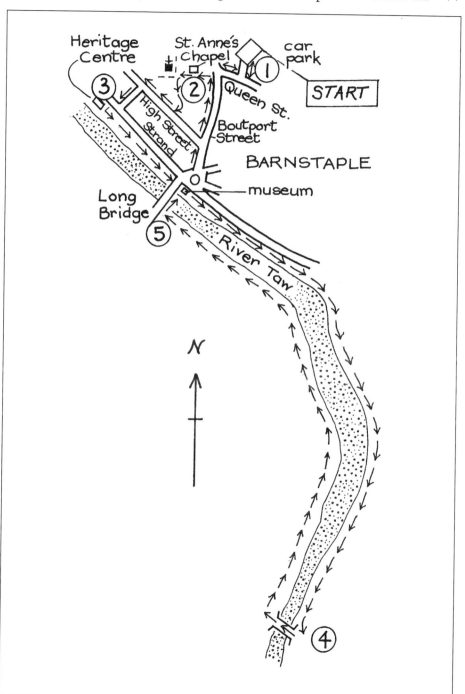

least some of the exiles may therefore have had contacts here. Or it may simply have been that, because Barnstaple was a thriving trading centre, there were many ships plying between North Devon and France and therefore more opportunities for the refugees to find passage with a Barnstaple vessel than one from another port. Whatever the reason, they certainly enriched the local community. They brought a host of talents with them; included among their number were silversmiths, dyers, weavers, clockmakers and many more. And they soon became integrated into society; one even served as mayor in the 18th century.

The Place

There are a number of places of interest along our route which have a bearing on Barnstaple's history, on the Huguenots in general and on our story in particular. The first is St Anne's Chapel. Originally a chantry chapel, where priests said prayers for those who donated money to the Church, it ceased to function as such after the Reformation and later became a school. Among its pupils was the playwright and poet John Gay, writer of *The Beggar's Opera*. From

St Anne's Chapel, Barnstaple

1685 to 1785 it was also used by the Huguenots for their Sunday services. It is now closed. Just across the lane from the chapel is the parish church, where Jacques and Elizabeth-Anne were married. It dates back to the 12th century, although most of the present structure is 14th century and the spire was added in the 16th century. Along the route, you also pass some delightful 17th century almshouses built by Thomas Horwood, a rich merchant, and a school established by his wife for 20 'poor maids'.

By the river, the Barnstaple Heritage Centre tells the story of the town, with a section on the Huguenots. The colonnade outside (known as Queen Anne's Walk) was where the merchants gathered and conducted much of their business. The centre is open on Monday to Saturday from 10 am to 5 pm between 1st April and 31st October, and Tuesday to Saturday from 10 am to 4.30 pm (3 pm on Saturday) for the rest of the year. And just beyond the Long Bridge is the Museum of Barnstaple and North Devon, which has more information and exhibits about the town and its surroundings, including a table carpet made in 1761 by Huguenot settlers for one of their number, Monier Roch, who became mayor of the town in that year. The museum is open Tuesday to Saturday between 10 am and 4.30 pm.

THE WALK

❶ Leave the Queen Street car park via Mallets Lane, and at the end turn right into Queen Street. Where the road bends to the right, turn left into Boutport Street, and then turn right just before the Rising Sun pub into Paternoster Row. St Anne's Chapel is on your right among the trees, and the parish church beyond it, on the other side of a pedestrian lane.

❷ Turn left into this lane (which is called Church Lane). You pass Horwood's Almshouses on your left and then, as the lane bends to the right, Alice Horwood's school, now a coffee house. It emerges into the modern bustle of High Street; turn right and

FOOD AND DRINK

There are pubs, restaurants and tearooms to suit all tastes in Barnstaple, but my recommendation, both for its charm and its situation (it is on the route of the walk, in the heart of the old town) is the Old School Coffee House in Alice Horwood's maids' school in Church Lane. It is licensed, and serves coffees, teas and lunches, with a wide range of fare, from sandwiches and ploughman's lunches to substantial main courses. Telephone: 01271 372793.

then left down Cross Street. This takes you down to the river, and the Heritage Centre is immediately opposite you.

❸ Turn left beyond the centre, to follow the brick path alongside the river. Go under the Long Bridge and you will find the Museum of Barnstaple and North Devon on your left as you emerge on the other side. Continue on the brick path, which comes out onto a road. When the road leaves the river, bear right, following the path alongside the river with a pretty park on your left, followed by a brief stretch of road and then some playing fields.

❹ The surfaced path ends at a disused railway bridge; go half-left to climb some steps and turn right along a new path to cross the bridge. Turn right again on the other side to follow the left bank of the river downstream. The path ends at a car park alongside a leisure centre; follow the pavement round to the right and you will come out at the Long Bridge.

❺ Turn right and cross the bridge. On the other side, take the second street on the left, which is Boutport Street. At the junction at the top, turn right into Queen Street and then left into Mallets Lane to return to the car park.

WALK 13
THE SECRET CHAPEL – LOUGHWOOD MEETING HOUSE

Length: 5¾ miles

The 'hidden' Loughwood Meeting House

GETTING THERE: Turn north off the A35 Honiton to Dorchester road just west of Axminster and follow the signs to Dalwood.

PARKING: There is some parking in the road in Dalwood, especially outside the church, but please ensure that you do not block any gateways or cause a bottleneck.

MAPS: OS Explorer 116 (formerly 29) Lyme Regis and Bridport; OS Landranger 193 Taunton and Lyme Regis (GR 247005; Loughwood Meeting House 252991).

INTRODUCTION

In the middle of the 17th century, Nonconformist worshippers, and particularly Baptists, were severely persecuted both by the authorities and by their fellow citizens – indeed, from 1661 until 1688 their meeting houses were illegal. They were ostracised, imprisoned,

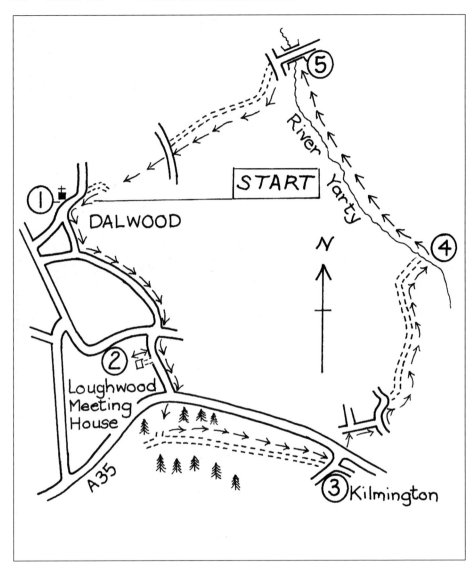

transported and sometimes even killed for their beliefs. This delightful walk takes you from the pretty village of Dalwood along quiet lanes, following the route worshippers would have taken to their 'hidden' meeting house in the 17th century. From Loughwood, you follow the route taken by the chapel's Kilmington contingent along a path and an old Roman road to Kilmington, and then return to Dalwood along farm tracks, green lanes and paths. Some of

Beckford Bridge, near Dalwood

the latter can become muddy after rain, so boots are strongly recommended. There are also a couple of fairly steep hills to negotiate, but the views from the top make the climbing worthwhile.

HISTORY

Loughwood Meeting House was built in dense woodland (since cleared), to help avoid detection by the authorities, and sentries were posted to warn of the approach of soldiers. It was apparently deliberately situated immediately on the boundary between Devon and what was then part of Dorset so that the preacher could escape into the neighbouring county if he was in danger of capture. Even after the Toleration Act of 1688 allowed meeting houses to function legally, the persecution of the Baptists continued. A story is told of how worshippers arrived for a service to find a huntsman standing in the pulpit blowing his horn while his dogs clambered over the pews. On another occasion they were met by a man standing in the doorway with his sword drawn, who threatened to run through anyone who tried to enter. One intrepid woman, however, just pushed past him, and he was left standing helpless while the rest of the congregation filed in.

THE PLACE

Loughwood Meeting House is a simple, fairly austere building down a farm track. Inside, however, it is a cheerful-looking place, with plain white walls, clear windows and bare pine woodwork. It is a National Trust property and is open all year round. It is not staffed and entry is free, but there is a box for donations towards its upkeep.

THE WALK

❶ The walk starts outside the church in the centre of Dalwood. Head west (right as you come out of the churchyard), and take the first turning on the left, which is Lower Lane. After about 300 yards you come to a junction; turn left. The lane now twists and turns and after about ½ mile emerges at a T-junction. Turn right and then immediately left into a fairly steep lane. After 150 yards you will come to Loughwood Farm; the meeting house is up a track on the right, opposite the farmhouse.

❷ After visiting the chapel, go back down the track and turn right to continue the walk. Climb up the lane to the A35. On the other side of the road you will see a public footpath sign. Cross the road carefully, as it is busy, and climb some steps into a wood. Follow a path alongside a bank until it meets a track; bear left and at the T-junction turn left again. You are now on the Roman road, which leads you straight into the village of Kilmington.

❸ Towards the end of the track you pass some houses and join Shute Road; bear left and turn immediately left again down Hill Crest. This takes you down to the A35 again; cross straight over to a drive. When the drive curves to the right, go straight on down a path which brings you to a lane. Turn right, and at the T-junction left. When the lane turns sharp left to Stockland bear right along a farm track, following the public footpath sign. Follow the track round to the left past the farm itself to a gate. Continue along

---

FOOD AND DRINK

For good food in delightful surroundings, call in at the Tucker's Arms in Dalwood at the end of your walk. It is a beautiful 13th century inn, and its specialities are fish, steak and game. Telephone: 01404 881342.

The Tucker's Arms, Dalwood

the track diagonally right across a field, crossing a stream via a footbridge in the middle. At the end you are faced with two gates; go through the left-hand one onto a track fringed by hedges. It enters a small wood and on the other side it forks; go right to a farm, crossing the River Yarty via a footbridge when you get there.

❹ Immediately on the other side, turn left, following the public footpath sign, and swing right round the buildings to a gate. Turn left on the other side and cross a field to a gateway. Cross the next field to a stile and the next to a gate. Go down to a footbridge across a small stream and bear right through a gap in a fence. Cross three more fields separated by a stile and a gateway. At the end of the third field there are two small gates separated by a footbridge, and you then follow the river to a stile leading into a lane.

❺ Turn left and cross a bridge. At the T-junction go straight on to a green lane, following the county 'unmetalled road' sign. There follows a long and fairly steep climb before the green lane emerges onto a surfaced track which leads to a lane. Turn left (signposted to Kilmington and Axminster). After about 50 yards turn right down a drive, following the public footpath sign. When the drive turns right to a house, go straight on down a path. When it reaches a bank, the path swings to the right and then to the left to cross a stile and then a footbridge into a field. Go straight across the field to a gate and keep to the right of the next field until you see a stile on your right; cross it and go straight down the next field to a gate. Keep to the left of the next field to a gate on the left. Go through and bear right along a lane. When it joins another lane, go straight on to cross a stream and return to the church on your right.

WALK 14
WRECKERS AND GHOSTS – THE HAUNTING OF CHAMBERCOMBE MANOR

Length: 3¾ miles

The corn mill at Hele

HOW TO GET THERE: Hele Bay is just east of Ilfracombe on the A399.

PARKING: There is a free car park at Hele Bay, on the right as you go down towards the beach. There is also a small car park at Chambercombe Manor if you want to start there.

MAPS: OS Explorer 139 Bideford, Ilfracombe and Barnstaple; OS Landranger 180 Barnstaple and Ilfracombe (GR 535476; Chambercombe Manor 532467).

INTRODUCTION

One of the less savoury activities of the people of North Devon during the 17th and 18th centuries was the practice of wrecking. One villain involved in this activity was William Oatway, who lived at

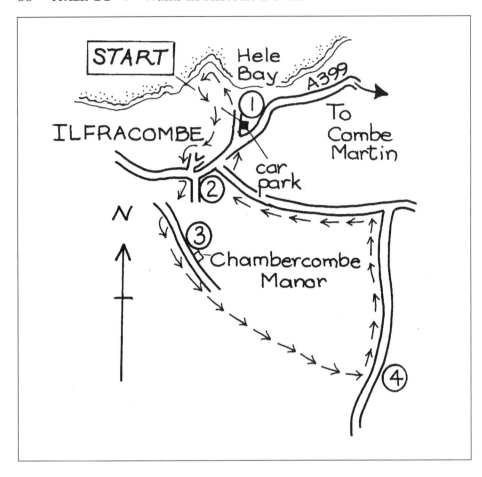

Chambercombe Manor in the 1700s. This is a delightfully varied walk which visits not only the charming and intriguing Chambercombe Manor but also the pretty little corn mill at Hele, and takes in a stretch of cliff path into the bargain. The views across the Bristol Channel to Wales are stunning, and the fields and hedgerows are ablaze with wild flowers in the spring and summer. There is a fairly steep climb up to the cliff at the start, which gives you a very good view of the kind of rugged coastline which made the old wreckers' task so easy, but if you would prefer to avoid it, a shorter route is given.

   I have chosen to start this walk at Hele Bay rather than at Chambercombe for two reasons. First, when the manor is closed, parking in the car park there is discouraged; and secondly, the car park is rather small, and on busy days it would be unfair to take up space there for two hours or more while walking. But if you do want to start the walk there, then simply begin at point 3 and finish with points 1 and 2.

HISTORY

Wrecking involved shining lights on the headlands along the coast in bad weather to confuse passing ships and lure them onto the rocks below. Any crew and passengers who were not drowned as a result were killed by the wreckers, who swarmed aboard the stricken vessel and stripped it of everything valuable. William Oatway combined wrecking with another popular pastime in coastal villages, smuggling. A tunnel has been discovered linking Chambercombe Manor with Hele Bay, and it is probable that it was used to bring booty and contraband up from the beach.

In 1865, the then tenant of the manor was making some repairs to the roof when he discovered a blocked-up window which he had not noticed before. He was puzzled, because he could not recall seeing a corresponding room in the house. He finally took a hammer to the nearest wall and broke through to find that there was indeed a room on the other side which had been completely sealed up. Not only that, on a bed in the room lay the skeleton of a woman. Several explanations have been put forward, but the most popular is that the woman was Kate Oatway, William's daughter. Married to an officer in Ireland, she was on her way to visit her parents when her father's gang lured her ship onto the rocks and she was killed with the rest of the passengers. Filled with remorse when he discovered what had happened, her father carried her up to the manor, laid her in her chamber and then bricked it up. It is said that she has haunted the house ever since her bones were disturbed.

THE PLACE

Chambercombe Manor dates back to the 11th century, and is mentioned in the Domesday Book, but it was significantly enlarged and altered in the 15th century, and there are also many later additions. It once belonged to the family of Lady Jane Grey, the poor girl who in 1553, at the age of 15, was made queen in an attempt to keep the Catholic Mary Tudor off the throne. She lasted just nine days, and was later beheaded for treason. The room next to the Haunted Room (where the skeleton was found) is called Lady Jane

The intriguing Chambercombe Manor

Grey's Room, but there is no firm evidence that she actually visited Chambercombe. The house is open between Easter Sunday and the end of September from 10.30 am to 5.30 pm Monday to Friday and from 2 pm to 5.30 pm on Sundays. It is closed on Saturdays. Visits are by guided tour only, and the tour takes an hour. Telephone 01271 862624.

THE WALK

(If you would prefer to avoid the climb to the cliff top, you can omit the first section by turning left out of the car park and at the top of the road going right along Watermouth Road. After just under ¼ mile turn left to join the main route.)

❶ On leaving the car park at Hele Bay, turn right towards the sea. Go to the left of the beach and climb some steps, following the Coast Path sign. At the junction at the top, go straight on, following the Coast Path sign again. At the next junction turn right, again following the Coast Path sign. The path continues to climb and wind along the cliff top. At the third junction, bear left off the Coast Path and start to descend gently. At the next junction go straight on and you will eventually join another path; bear right (signposted to Ilfracombe). After about 50 yards you come to a fork; follow the broad track on the left and go through a gate onto a road. At the bottom go right into Hillside Road and after a few yards you will come to Watermouth Road, the main A399. Turn sharp left, and after a few yards right, following the public footpath sign.

> **FOOD AND DRINK**
>
> The Hele Bay Hotel, on the corner above the car park, offers sustenance of all kinds, from tea and coffee to a range of alcoholic and non-alcoholic drinks, and from sandwiches and baguettes to main meals and specials such as deep-fried Camembert and stuffed chicken breasts, all in a congenial atmosphere. Telephone: 01271 867795.

❷ Turn immediately right again up a narrow track, which narrows to a path as it climbs. It runs high above a valley and emerges onto a lane; turn left. This lane takes you down to Chambercombe Manor.

❸ When you have visited the manor, continue along the lane (ie turn left as you come out of the gate) to a stableyard. Go through the yard to a gate. Bear left on the other side – there is a signpost but it is all but illegible. This takes you to a path and then a track running up the valley. The track can become muddy at times, as it gets churned up by passing livestock. Go through a gate into a field and follow the grassy track on the other side as it climbs up a hill to another gate. Cross the next field to a third gate, and go through the farmyard beyond to a surfaced track which climbs up out of the valley. It crosses a field and leads, via a cattle grid, to a lane.

❹ Turn left. After about ¾ mile you come to a T-junction; turn left again. The lane descends steeply towards Hele Bay and Ilfracombe. At the bottom you will find a track on your right marked with a public footpath sign and a sign to the old corn mill and pottery. Turn off here and follow the path through the mill complex. It emerges on the main road; cross over to the road on the other side and the car park on the right.

WALK 15
'THE KING OF THE BEGGARS' – BAMPFYLDE MOORE CAREW OF BICKLEIGH

Length: 3¾ miles

Bickleigh Castle

HOW TO GET THERE: Bickleigh Castle is just west of the A396 Exeter to Tiverton road near where it crosses the River Exe about 3 miles south of Tiverton. Turn off onto the A3072 Crediton road, and it is signposted left from there. Bickleigh village is on the other side of the A396 and is signposted from it.

PARKING: There is parking at Bickleigh Castle. If the castle is closed, and if you are planning on taking refreshments at the Fisherman's Cot alongside the river, you can ask if you can leave your car there while you walk and start the walk from point 4. Otherwise, park in the road in Bickleigh village and start at point 3.

MAPS: OS Explorer 114 Exeter and the Exe Valley; OS Landranger 192 Exeter and Sidmouth (GR 936067).

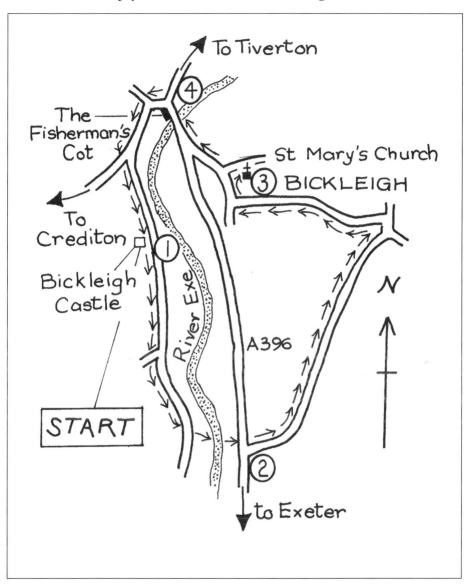

INTRODUCTION

Bickleigh's most famous son in the 18th century was Bampfylde Moore Carew, 'King of the Beggars' – a well-born rogue who was a master of disguise and lived a colourful life. This walk explores the delights of the beautiful Exe valley, taking in historic Bickleigh Castle, where the hero of our story (if one can call him that!) grew up, and the pretty village of Bickleigh, where he is buried. For the most part it follows deserted, flower-filled lanes, although there is one short stretch of farmland to cross and a suspension bridge across the river. There is also one short but fairly steep climb towards the end.

HISTORY

Bickleigh Castle came into the possession of the Carew family in the 16th century, and they held it for almost four centuries, until 1922. They were one of the most important families in the south-west of England. In the 17th century, however, the heiress to the castle married a distant cousin who lived near Newton Abbot, and from then on it was usually used by younger sons who served as Rectors of Bickleigh.

One such, who was Rector in the late 17th and early 18th centuries, was the father of Bampfylde Moore Carew. Young Bampfylde was educated at Blundell's School in nearby Tiverton but ran away from there to join a band of gypsies. Soon he had learned all they could teach him about begging and trickery, and embarked on his own career as a vagabond. He appeared all over South Devon in a variety of guises – a shipwrecked mariner, a madman, an impoverished miller, a farmer who had lost all his cattle, a clergyman who had resigned his living over a matter of conscience, a one-legged tinminer, even a widow. He once extracted money from some friends three times in succession, in three different disguises, without arousing their suspicions. In 1733 he married Mary Gray, the daughter of a Newcastle surgeon, and they had a baby girl, but this did not deter him. He continued his vagabond life, but in 1739 he was arrested and imprisoned. He was then handed over to an Exeter merchant, who shipped him off to America to be sold as a slave. He managed to escape, found refuge with some Indians and then took up his old trade of begging to raise his passage home.

On his return, he was treated as something of a celebrity by both rich and poor, and counted many of the aristocracy among his friends (including several of his own relatives, who might have been expected to reject such a rogue). He was well aware of his fame. Once, when he was begging outside a doctor's house, the maid brought him a halfpenny. Rejecting it contemptuously, he said, 'I am no halfpenny man, but Bampfylde Moore Carew, the King of the Beggars'. Upon which the doctor himself came to the door and gave

St Mary's church

him sixpence. His old master caught up with him soon after his return and he was captured and shipped back to America again – only to escape once more. He was arrested soon after his return and spent another six months in prison, after which he seems to have given up the vagabond's trade. The reason is not clear, but remorse for his wickedness seems to have played a part. He was given a pension by one of his relatives, but it is also said that he won a large sum of money in a lottery, which must have eased his retirement considerably. He returned to Bickleigh, where he died in 1758. He is buried at his father's church in the village.

THE PLACE

Bickleigh Castle is actually a moated manor house rather than a castle as such. Its chapel dates back to the 11th century, but most of the house was rebuilt in the 15th century. It was a Royalist stronghold in the Civil War, and there are arms and armour from that period on display. It is open during Easter week (Good Friday to Friday) and on Wednesdays, Sundays and bank holidays from then until May, and daily from June to early October (except Saturdays)

2 pm to 5.30 pm. Telephone 01884 855363 for more details.

St Mary's church, in the village, is mainly 14th century. Look out for the Carew monuments, which date from the 16th and 17th centuries. Bampfylde Moore Carew is buried at the southeast end.

THE WALK

❶ Turn right from Bickleigh Castle and follow the lane for a little over ½ mile to a junction; go straight on. Having left the river at Bickleigh Castle, the lane now swings left to rejoin it. It soon swings right again, and you will see the entrance to Tray Mill Farm on your left. Turn off here and go through the farmyard to a gate. Cross the field beyond to a suspension bridge. Cross a track on the other side and go through a kissing gate; go diagonally right across the field beyond to another kissing gate in the fence on your right. Turn left on the other side and go through a gate onto the main road.

❷ Cross the road to a lane (signposted to Butterleigh). Follow this lane for a little over a mile and you will find a lane leading off to the right; go straight on but turn left after a few yards up the next lane. It climbs steeply for a while and then begins to descend. At the bottom, on the edge of Bickleigh, is a T-junction; turn right. When you come to the Old Bakery on the left, turn right up a track. This leads to a path, which comes out at a drive and then a lane which leads to the church.

❸ At the end of the lane turn left and at the junction go straight on. This lane emerges onto a bend in the main A396. As you join the main road, you will see a small side road going off to the right; follow that past Bickleigh Mill Country Living Centre until it joins the A396 again just before Bickleigh Bridge. Cross the bridge with care, as this is a busy road.

❹ You pass the Fisherman's Cot and then turn left along the A3072 (signposted to Crediton and Bickleigh Castle). Cross another little river and at the junction follow the main road round to the left (still signposted to Crediton and Bickleigh

FOOD AND DRINK

The Fisherman's Cot is an attractive thatched inn beside Bickleigh Bridge, with a beautiful large garden by the riverside. It offers breakfasts, coffees, lunches, teas and evening meals, with an excellent carvery and a good range of snacks and other dishes. Telephone: 01884 855237.

Castle). After another 200 yards, turn left down a lane, following the sign to Bickleigh Castle. The lane goes through a wood, following the river, and after about 600 yards you will find Bickleigh Castle on your right.

WALK 16
THE SCOURGE OF THE EXCISEMEN – JACK RATTENBURY OF BEER

Length: 4¼ miles

Great Seaside, Branscombe

HOW TO GET THERE: Turn south off the A3052 between Sidmouth and Seaton and follow the B3174 to Beer.

PARKING: Follow the signs for the Beer village centre until you come to a sign pointing right to the car park. Do not follow the first car park sign, but turn left up The Meadows, following the second sign.

MAPS: OS Explorer 116 (formerly 29) Lyme Regis and Bridport (start and finish), 115 (formerly 30) Exmouth and Sidmouth (middle section); OS Landranger 192 Exeter and Sidmouth (GR 228887; Beer Quarry Caves 214893).

INTRODUCTION
In the 18th and early 19th centuries, smuggling was a major source

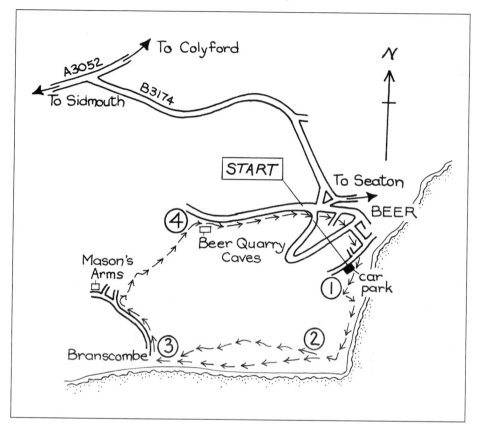

of income in the villages along Devon's south coast – indeed, along with quarrying and fishing, it was the mainstay of Beer's economy. And the best known of these smugglers was Jack Rattenbury. The first part of this walk takes you along the Coast Path to the pretty village of Branscombe, with superb sea views along the way. You then cut inland along pleasant farm and woodland paths to Beer Quarry Caves, where the smugglers hid their contraband, and return to Beer via lanes and village paths. There is some steep climbing out of Branscombe, halfway round, but otherwise the going is relatively easy.

History
The cliffs around Beer provided perfect shelter for smugglers to land their contraband, and the extensive network of caves at the nearby quarry provided an ideal place in which to hide it – it was a brave

exciseman who would venture into the dark maze of tunnels and galleries. It has even been said that there was a secret passage from the quarry to the cliffs, but no trace of it has been found.

Not all those involved in the smuggling trade were brigands and ruffians – the lords and parsons were also said to have been involved, and for many impoverished quarrymen and fishermen it was the only way they could feed their families adequately. Having said that, those at the sharp end were none too squeamish in their dealings with authority – one exciseman fell mysteriously from Beer Head, while another managed to drown in three inches of water in Beer Brook after supposedly falling off his horse. It is hardly surprising that few were prepared to search the quarry too diligently.

Jack Rattenbury, born in 1778, led an interesting and varied life. He was pressed into the Navy after being tried for smuggling, but deserted and returned to his old trade. He managed to evade capture until gout forced him to retire and from then on he led a peaceful and law-abiding life, helped by a pension from Lord Rolle, the local lord of the manor, who appears to have been involved with Rattenbury during his smuggling career (as confirmed by the existence of a secret chamber at his lordship's Bovey House which was specially adapted for storing contraband). As if to cock a final snook at the establishment, Rattenbury published his memoirs after his retirement, in which he described his methods and career in some detail.

THE PLACE

Beer stone is an ideal material for stonemasons; when newly dug it is soft and easy to work but when exposed to the elements it hardens and wears well. The workings which are now Beer Quarry Caves supplied stone to the Romans, the Saxons and the Normans, and continued to be exploited until the beginning of the 20th century.

The result of all these centuries of quarrying is an immense network of tunnels, caves and galleries supported by enormous pillars, in which the styles and methods used in the different eras can clearly be distinguished. It covers an area the equivalent of eleven football pitches, and one can see, as one explores even the relatively small area that is open to the public, what a superb hiding place it was for the smugglers' wares. There is even a chapel in which Catholics worshipped during times of persecution.

The complex is open from Easter to the end of October, and there

Beer Quarry Caves

are hour-long guided tours starting at 10 am (11 am in October), with the last tour at 5 pm (4 pm in October). The caves are fairly chilly (12°C), so jumpers or coats are recommended, whatever the conditions on the surface. Dogs are not allowed underground.

THE WALK

❶ Go down to the bottom of the car park and turn right to join the Coast Path (signposted to Branscombe). When you reach the entrance to a caravan park go left, following the coast path sign. Go through a kissing gate into a field, and then through a gap in a line of trees into another field. This is followed by four more kissing gates and four more fields.

❷ Eventually, about ¾ mile after leaving the car park, you come to a path junction and are faced with a choice; you can either go left and follow the Coast Path just above the beach or you can continue straight on along the cliff top. There is no difference in distance, but my personal preference is to take the clifftop route, as it enables one to enjoy the lovely coastal views for longer. The climb down the cliff side is also rather steep.

If you take the lower route, you will find it quite straight-forward; there are no deviations or other paths to confuse you. If you are taking the upper route, you go through another kissing gate and then come to a path junction. Go straight on, following the sign to Branscombe. Go through another gate and go straight on (again signposted to Branscombe). At the next junction follow the yellow footpath waymark down the hill. Keep to the left and go down some steps to a gate to rejoin the Coast Path. Cross a track and go down to a gate leading into a lane.

❸ Turn right and follow the lane up the hill. At the junction, go right to follow the main route, or straight on if you want to stop at the Mason's Arms. After a few yards turn off right, following the

> **FOOD AND DRINK**
>
> The Mason's Arms is a very attractive pub just a few hundred yards off the route in Branscombe with a wide-ranging menu – from sandwiches and ploughman's lunches to light meals such as chicken and smoked bacon terrine and a variety of tempting main courses, including spicy crab cakes.
> Telephone: 01297 680300.

The Mason's Arms, Branscombe

public footpath sign. Go up some steps and after a steep hill you come to a stile, after which the climb becomes less strenuous.

At the fork, go straight on, and at the next fork, after a few yards, go straight on again (signposted to Beer). The path now runs through a wood. At the next junction, follow the main path round to the right (signposted to Beer again). Cross a stile into a field. At the path junction at the end of the field, go through a gate and go diagonally left across the next field. Cross a stile and then a track, and go diagonally left again across the next field. Cross another stile and follow the path among some trees. After a while you will find a stile on your right; cross it and after a few yards cross another one into a wood. When you come to a track, turn right and cross the car park to reach the Beer Quarry Caves.

❹ When you leave the caves, turn right at the car park and right again at the road. After about ½ mile this brings you to Beer. Continue along it until you reach Mare Lane on the right. Turn up it, and when it goes to the right after 200 yards or so, turn left, following the footpath sign to the village and the beach. The path emerges onto a road; turn left and immediately right onto another path (again signposted to the village and beach). Go down some steps and at the next road cross over to a small lane, following the public footpath sign. At the end go straight on along the path which eventually brings you to another road. Turn right and at the junction, bear left into the car park.

SIR THOMAS TYRWHITT'S DREAM – PRINCETOWN AND THE PLYMOUTH-DARTMOOR RAILWAY

Length: 5½ miles

The High Moorland Visitor Centre, Princetown

HOW TO GET THERE: The B3212 goes through the village, which can also be approached from the B3357 Tavistock to Ashburton road.	**PARKING:** There is a public car park behind The High Moorland Visitor Centre, in the centre of the village.	**MAPS:** OS Outdoor Leisure 28 Dartmoor; OS Landranger 191 Okehampton and North Dartmoor (GR 589735).

INTRODUCTION

Sir Thomas Tyrwhitt, a personal friend of the Prince Regent, later George IV, who lived at Tor Royal near what is now Princetown, had a dream: to open up and 'civilise' central Dartmoor, making it a hub

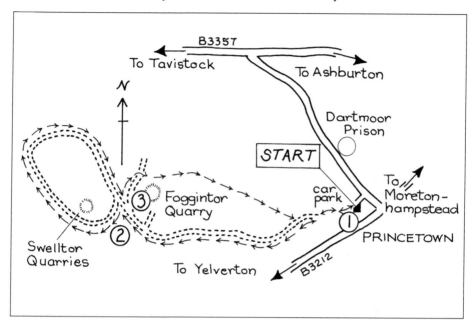

of agriculture and industry. This undemanding ramble gives you a taste of Dartmoor without too much effort. It follows the track of the old Plymouth–Dartmoor Railway, part of Sir Thomas's plan for the area, past the remains of Princetown's granite quarries before branching off to trace a much older route – the Tavistock to Ashburton packhorse trail, which was used by traders in medieval times. The views across the wide spaces of the northern moor are superb.

HISTORY

The first stages of Tyrwhitt's plan went well; he founded Princetown (named after the Prince Regent) as the centre of his new community at the end of the 18th century, and granite quarries were opened nearby at about the same time. He also persuaded the government to build a new prison there for French prisoners from the Napoleonic Wars, and the first prisoners and their guards arrived in 1809.

He did not have the same success with the rest of his project, however. He believed that he could make the moorland soil productive by mixing in limestone and sea sand, and that settlers would then be attracted to the area by its agricultural potential. He set up a company to build a railway from Plymouth to Princetown, the aim being to use it to import the fertilising materials and the settlers' other supplies, and to export granite from the quarries and produce from the newly established farms. He soon discovered, however, that the moor could not be made fertile simply by the application of limestone and sand, and the cornerstone of his project had to be abandoned. As a result, the railway's traffic was almost all one way: it carried granite down to Plymouth but on the return journey the trucks were almost empty – hardly a profitable arrangement. The company went through a number of financial crises, and the first dividend was not declared until 1870, 47 years after the line was opened – and then it was a mere five shillings per £100 share. The line was upgraded and became part of the Great Western system in 1883.

Although Princetown's population continued to grow, it never became the productive centre that Tyrwhitt envisaged, owing its continued existence mainly to the quarries and the prison. The latter closed in 1816, when the last remaining prisoners were released, but reopened in 1850 as a civilian establishment, and it continues to dominate the village to this day. The quarries have long-since ceased operation, and the railway was closed in 1956. Today, Princetown's economy relies mainly on the prison and the tourist trade.

THE PLACE

Dartmoor Prison provides a gloomy, almost menacing backdrop to Princetown, but there is much else to interest the visitor in and around the village. The old Duchy Hotel has been converted into the High Moorland Visitor Centre (open every day except Christmas Day, Boxing Day and New Year's Day), which has a free exhibition of Dartmoor's history, wildlife and economy. The disused quarries to the west, which supplied granite for many of London's major Victorian buildings and monuments, are also full of interest and wildlife; along the dismantled railway near Swelltor Quarry, for example, you can see a number of beautifully carved corbels which were cut for the construction of London Bridge, but were found to be surplus to requirements and just left beside the track.

THE WALK

❶ Leave the car park via the vehicle entrance and turn left. Follow the road past the fire station and turn left just beyond it onto a path signposted 'disused railway'. Follow the path round to the right and

Corbels cut for London Bridge but not used, near Swelltor Quarries

through a gate. You soon join a track, which is the route of Sir Thomas's railway. It is a clear and easy track which takes you out onto the open moor.

❷ After about 1¼ miles you will come to a junction. Go straight on, and take the left fork soon afterwards. After about 200 yards you will come to a path leading off to the left; turn off, and where the path you are on crosses a track to climb the hill ahead, turn left. This will take you round the bottom of Swelltor Quarry. You can branch off to the right and go inside if you wish. You are now back on a branch of the dismantled

FOOD AND DRINK

There are several places in Princetown where visitors can refresh themselves. My personal recommendations are: the Plume of Feathers Inn, a delightful pub on the main road which offers a warm welcome and a wide range of food in a traditional setting, from steaks and curries to ploughman's lunches and jacket potatoes. Telephone: 01822 890240; and Lord's tearooms and restaurant, opposite the High Moorland Visitor Centre, which is open for morning coffee, lunch and teas, including their famous Devon cream tea.Telephone: 01822 890707.

railway; a little way beyond the quarry entrance you will find the corbels beside the track on your right. Follow the railway line all the way round to the right, circling King's Tor. Soon you will see the spoil heaps of Foggintor Quarry ahead of you.

❸ When you come to a junction in the track, a little over ½ mile from King's Tor, go left towards the quarry. When you reach it, go between the ruined buildings on your left and the quarry entrance on your right. Once past the quarry, leave the track and bear right across the moor towards the tall mast you can see on North Hessary Tor, on the horizon. As you go towards it, you will cross a line of stone markers for the ancient Tavistock to Ashburton packhorse trail, each inscribed with a 'T' (for 'Tavistock') on one side and 'A' (for 'Ashburton') on the other. Turn right and follow the markers across the moor. After about ¾ mile you will come to the disused railway again; turn left and follow it back to Princetown. (Alternatively, if the visibility is not very good and you are worried about losing your way, you can go straight up to the mast and turn right onto the clear path which leads straight back to Princetown.)

WALK 18
ABBOT VONIER'S VISION –
BUCKFAST ABBEY

Length: 5½ miles

Buckfast Abbey

HOW TO GET THERE: Turn off the A38 Exeter to Plymouth road at the Dart Bridge exit (signposted to Buckfastleigh if you are approaching from the north, to Buckfast if you are coming from the south). Follow the signs to Buckfast and Buckfast Abbey.

PARKING: There is parking at the Abbey for those visiting the complex.

MAPS: OS Outdoor Leisure 28 Dartmoor; OS Landranger 202 Torbay and South Dartmoor (GR 740672).

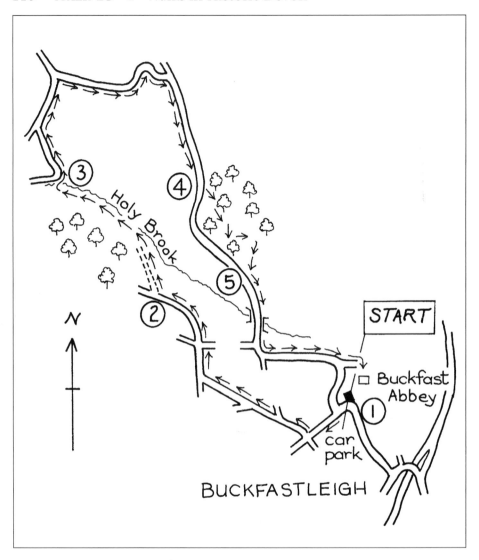

INTRODUCTION

The 11th century abbey church at Buckfast was rebuilt in the early 20th century through the vision and endeavour of Abbot Vonier, and is today a magnificent memorial to his faith. This walk starts by following lanes out of Buckfast along the route that was taken by the monks of old when they had to cross Dartmoor to visit their colleagues at Tavistock Abbey. It then alternates between more quiet lanes with flower-filled hedgerows and beautiful woods. You also have the opportunity to visit Hembury Castle, an Iron Age hill fort, along the way. There are one or two hills to climb, but they are generally short and not too steep.

HISTORY

The original Buckfast Abbey was founded in 1018, during the reign of King Knut (Canute), and was endowed with extensive lands. It was abolished in 1539, however, as part of Henry VIII's dissolution of the monasteries, and the abbey buildings were gradually demolished by the new owners.

The Roman Catholic Church acquired the site again towards the end of the 19th century, and in 1882 the first monks arrived to re-establish the community. But the rebuilding of the magnificent abbey church had to wait until the beginning of the 20th century, and was only undertaken at all because of the vision of the community's leader, Abbot Vonier.

The foundations of the medieval church were found under what was then the monks' vegetable garden, and the Abbot decided that a new church, equally beautiful, would be built on the same site. It is said that the project started with a sovereign and a horse and cart. One of the monks was trained as a stonemason, and he was given four or five others to assist him. The building took 32 years, from 1906 to 1938, and the Abbot lived just long enough to see his vision become reality – he died within weeks of the church's completion.

THE PLACE

Buckfast Abbey is now a major complex. Apart from the church (and the monks' accommodation, which is, of course, not open to the public), there is a gift shop, a bookshop, a restaurant, an exhibition centre and a shop selling produce from monasteries around Europe. It is open throughout the year, and entry is free apart from the exhibition. The main attraction, however, must be the magnificent church, which dominates the area. At the end of the original building, behind the altar, is a modern chapel with the most stunning stained glass window, also made by the monks.

THE WALK

❶ Leave the car park and turn right (signposted to Buckfastleigh and Holne). Follow the road up a hill, ignoring the turning to the right to Buckfast, and at the crossroads at the top turn right (signposted to

Buckfast Abbey church which took 32 years to build

The remains of the medieval fort inside Hembury Castle

Holne and Scorriton). At the next junction, go straight on (signposted to Holne and Scorriton again), and at the next two, go straight on again. The next junction is a crossroads; go straight on again, still following the sign to Holne and Scorriton.

❷ About 600 yards beyond the crossroads you will see a house called Burchetts Lodge on your right; turn right up a track just before it, and pass the house to a gate. Continue along the track into a wood on the other side, and at the fork go right. At the next fork go straight on and at the third take the more definite of the two branches, which goes straight on again, along the edge of the wood. The track narrows to a path and you will see a stream below you on your right.

❸ At the end of the wood you cross a footbridge and emerge onto a lane; turn right. The lane climbs steeply to a T-junction; turn right again (signposted to Holne). At the next junction, about ¼ mile further on, turn right (signposted to Shuttaford). The lane winds into a valley and then climbs out again to a T-junction. Turn right.

❹ After about 700 yards you will come to a car park on your left, with a gate leading into Hembury Woods. Turn off and go through the gate. On the other side, take the path that goes straight on. It will bring you to another gate; on the other side you will cross the outer ditch of Hembury Castle and enter the hill fort itself. Straight ahead you will find a mound, which is all that remains of a medieval fort which was built within the Iron Age defences. Go left from there and follow the clear path down to cross the outer ditch again to a stile. Follow the path down the hill on the other side. After a few yards you will come to a fork; go left, following the arrow on the post pointing to the car park. Further down the path crosses a track; go straight on, again following the arrow to the car park. At the next track go right (still following the car park arrow).

❺ After a short distance you emerge onto a lane; turn left. The lane takes you down a hill to cross a river, and about 200 yards later you come to a T-junction. Turn left, and after a few yards you will come to another junction; follow the main lane round to the left (signposted to Buckfast). At the next junction (with a road called Hembury Park), go straight on. At the next (Higher Mill Lane), go straight on again. At the end, go through an archway on your right to enter the abbey complex. (Note: Dogs are not allowed in the abbey complex, so if you have one with you, you should turn right up Higher Mill Lane and at the T-junction at the top of the hill turn left to avoid the complex and return to the car park.)

FOOD AND DRINK

The Grange Restaurant in the abbey complex is a self-service establishment offering a delicious range of fare, from sandwiches and rolls to salads and hot meals, as well as cream teas, cakes etc. Telephone: 01364 642304.

WALK 19
PREPARATIONS FOR D-DAY –
SLAPTON SANDS

Length: 5¾ miles

The monument to those killed during D-Day exercises, Torcross

HOW TO GET THERE: The walk starts at the memorial on the A379 between Dartmouth and Kingsbridge, just a few yards north of the turn-off to Slapton village.

PARKING: There is a large car park about 50 yards south of the memorial, on the other side of the Slapton turn-off. If that is full, you can park at Torcross, further south, and start the walk from there (point 5 in the route description).

MAPS: OS Outdoor Leisure 20 South Devon; OS Landranger 202 Torbay and South Dartmoor (GR 829443; Torcross monument 823422).

INTRODUCTION

In November 1943, the people of the South Hams received a shock: from Blackawton and Slapton, from East Allington and Stokenham, everyone was to be evacuated. Farmers were to abandon their crops, fishermen their nets; the old, the infirm, the young, all were called upon to leave within six weeks. The reason was that the 3-mile stretch of Slapton Sands was the ideal place for the American forces to practise amphibious landings in preparation for the assault on the Normandy beaches. This walk takes you through three of the picturesque villages that were evacuated as well as visiting two memorials associated with the D-Day preparations. It also takes in a magnificent beach, a beautiful wood, quiet lanes and a freshwater lake, plus outstanding coastal views and wild flowers galore. There is some climbing along the way, but none of it is too strenuous and the views make the effort worthwhile.

HISTORY

The whole of the area around Slapton was taken over by the US Army in December 1943 and D-Day exercises began early in 1944. Ten years later, the American authorities erected a memorial on Slapton Sands to express their gratitude to the local residents for their co-operation in evacuating their homes.

That was not the end of the story, however. There had been vague rumours during and after the war of 'accidents' during the D-Day rehearsals, but nothing specific was known. Then a local man, Ken Small, found a disturbing amount of military equipment which had been washed up on the beach – cap badges, spent bullets, mines etc. He sensed that the 'accidents' that had been reported were just the tip of a somewhat bigger iceberg. And when an American tank was found on the sea bed, suspicion turned to certainty. Small had the tank brought to shore, where it was installed in 1984 as a memorial to those who had lost their lives in the exercises. Convinced that the authorities were hiding something, he persisted in his enquiries, only to be met with bureaucratic insensitivity, procrastination and denial. Finally, however, he arrived at the truth: on 28th April 1944 German gunboats had stumbled on a landing exercise in progress and as many as 749 American servicemen had lost their lives.

Exactly 50 years after the tragedy, in 1994, a memorial service was held on the Sands to commemmorate their sacrifice. But it is only because of one man's insistence that they should be acknowledged, and his refusal to be fobbed off, that the great wrong done to their memory by the authorities was righted.

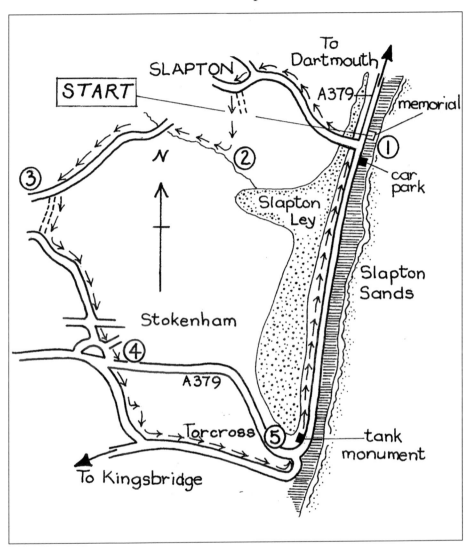

THE PLACE

Walking along Slapton Sands, it is easy to see why this part of the coast was chosen for the D-Day exercises. Stretching for 3 miles, the beach must have been ideally suited to amphibious training, and one can almost visualise the activity that the exercises entailed. And to add to the attraction of the scene there is Slapton Ley on the other side of the spit, a nature reserve and an internationally recognised haven for birds.

Approximately halfway along the beach is the memorial erected by the American authorities – a simple stone obelisk bearing a message of thanks to the local villagers for their co-operation. And at the southern end, in the Torcross car park, is the tank which was lifted from the sea bed and which stands as a stark memorial to all the servicemen who lost their lives in the exercises and whose sacrifice was unrecognised for so long, not least by their own government. Next to it there are now memorial plaques belatedly put up by the authorities. And you may find Ken Small, the man whose persistence made it all possible, selling signed copies of his book about the episode and his quest for the truth, *The Forgotten Dead*, from the boot of his car alongside.

THE WALK

❶ From the memorial go south beside the main road for a short distance and turn right down the lane leading to Slapton village. Follow it into the village, and at the junction where it turns sharp right (signposted to Totnes), go left. (For the Tower Inn follow the Totnes road round to the right and you will find the pub on your right.) Follow the lane down a hill and then up another one. It swings to the right, and soon after it does so you will see a lane going off to the left, signposted to Kimberley Nurseries, and with a public footpath sign pointing to Slapton Ley. Follow that. It soon becomes a track and goes through a gate and alongside a field on the other side. At the end of the field, go through a wooden gate next to the entrance to a water treatment works and follow the path on the other side.

❷ When you get to the bottom, turn right (signposted to Deer Bridge). You pass some reed beds on your left, with a wood on your right, and after about 600 yards emerge onto a lane. Turn left and at the junction follow the main lane across a bridge. It swings right and begins to climb.

FOOD AND DRINK
There are six pubs to choose from on this walk: two in Slapton, two in Stokenham and two in Torcross. My favourite, however, is the Tower Inn in Slapton, just a short way off the route of this walk. It is a most attractive old pub, full of character, and offers a good range of fare, from sandwiches and ploughman's lunches to soups, steaks and vegetarian specialities. Telephone: 01548 580216.

❸ After a little over ½ mile you will come to a track leading off to

The American memorial to the evacuated villagers, Slapton Sands

the left, signposted 'Scrubs Lane to Frittiscombe'. Turn down it and at the fork go right to pass to the right of a barn. Go through a farmyard to reach a surfaced lane; turn left. The lane climbs and after ½ mile you will reach the village of Stokenham. At the T-junction go right and then immediately left. At the next T-junction, at the bottom of the hill, turn left and at the next junction follow the main lane round to the right to pass the church and come out at the main road.

❹ Turn right and immediately left up a lane. It climbs steadily and after about ¼ mile you will see a plank bridge across a stream on your left. Cross that and climb some steps to a stile, and then some more steps into a wood. Follow the path to the right and then to the left. Shortly after the left-hand bend you will see a low-level sign pointing straight on to the viewpoint. At this point you need to turn right and follow the less clear path straight up the hill. At the next junction go straight on, following the low-level sign pointing to the main gate. At the end of the wood, go through a kissing gate back into the lane and turn left. After about 150 yards you will come to a T-junction; turn left. After another ½ mile or so, you begin to descend into Torcross.

❺ At the bottom you meet the main road; go straight on and you will find the monument to the men killed in the D-Day exercises in the car park on the left. At the other end of the car park there is also a hide from which you can watch the bird life on Slapton Ley.

From here you have a choice: you can go through a gap in the fence at the end of the car park to follow a path alongside Slapton Ley or cross the road and walk along the beach. After about 1¼ miles the path comes out onto the lane leading to Slapton village; turn right to return to the car park. If you have been walking along the beach, the car park is on the left after a similar distance.

WALK 20
THE GREAT FLOOD – LYNMOUTH

Length: 4½ miles

Lynmouth

HOW TO GET THERE:
Lynmouth is on the A39
between Minehead and
Barnstaple.

PARKING: There are two car
parks in Lynmouth, one at the
bottom of the village, at the
end of The Esplanade, and
another at the top, just off
the A39. The former is the
better for this walk, as it
enables you to explore the
village as you go. There is
also free parking in Riverside
Road, the main street, but in
summer this is time-
restricted.

MAPS: OS Outdoor Leisure 9
Exmoor; OS Landranger 180
Barnstaple and Ilfracombe
(GR 720497).

INTRODUCTION

The area around Lynmouth was called the little Switzerland of England in the 19th century because of its beautiful scenery and quiet charm, but in August 1952 the East Lyn River became a raging torrent that swept through the village, leaving death and destruction in its wake.

This stunning walk explores the densely wooded valley of the East Lyn and the Cleaves (steep hillsides) above it. Some of the views will take your breath away (you can see the mountains of mid-Wales on a clear day) and the riverside paths are an absolute delight. There is some steep climbing at the start of the walk, but otherwise the going is easy.

HISTORY

Lynmouth is an old fishing village, some of whose cottages date back to the 14th century. Because of its charm and the beauty of the

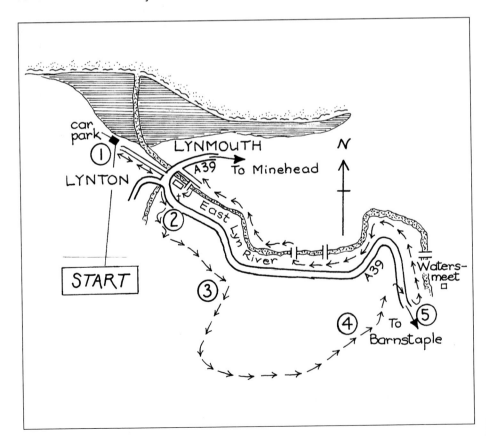

surrounding countryside, it became very popular with holidaymakers during the 19th century. One of its visitors at that time was the poet Percy Bysshe Shelley. During his few months in the village he wrote a number of seditious tracts, railing against the establishment. He put these into bottles which he launched into the sea, presumably hoping that they would be washed up and read further along the coast without being traced back to him. However, the authorities got wind of his activities and he had to make a hasty escape across the Bristol Channel to Wales to avoid the local justices.

Apart from this brief flurry of excitement, Lynmouth led a fairly quiet existence until 1952. In that year, however, its peace was shattered in a particularly brutal way. Torrential rain fell on the uplands of Exmoor on the night of 15th/16th August. Because the topsoil on the moor is a mere 9 inches deep, and the subsoil is a hard, compact, iron pan, very little of the water could be absorbed, and in one night some 300 million gallons rushed off the high ground into the East Lyn River. The river became a raging, murderous flood, bursting its banks and destroying everything in its path. Along the valley above Lynmouth, the whole hamlet of Midham was wiped out, and 28 bridges in the area were washed away or damaged. The main casualty, however, was Lynmouth itself. The river simply crushed any buildings in its path. Thirty-one people lost their lives that night, and 93 houses were destroyed or had subsequently to be demolished. As can be imagined, the effect on such a small, close-knit community was devastating.

THE PLACE

The cottage in which Shelley stayed during his sojourn in Lynmouth, opposite the church, was one of those destroyed during the floods, but enough of the original buildings in the village remain or have been restored to make this one of the prettiest coastal villages in Devon. It is difficult now to imagine the devastation that must have faced the survivors on that August morning, but there is a memorial to the flood victims in the church, and overlooking the harbour is the Memorial Hall, erected in 1958 in memory of those who lost their lives. The museum in Lynmouth's twin village of Lynton also has a display about the flood.

Although the valley of the East Lyn is now normally beautifully tranquil, the path alongside the river passes the foundations of houses destroyed in the tragedy. Also look out for a stone bottle set

Lynmouth church

into a rock by the path to commemorate the Lynrock Mineral Water Company, which was also destroyed.

THE WALK

❶ Leave the car park and walk back up Lynmouth's main street (Riverside Road) to the main A39, passing the Memorial Hall as you go. Turn right and then immediately left. You will find the church on your left.

❷ Immediately opposite the church, turn right onto a surfaced path which winds up between whitewashed cottages. It is a steep climb, and as you leave the village, you enter a wood. You will come to a point where a path goes straight on while the broad track you are on swings sharp right; take the latter, and follow it as it winds through the wood. At the next fork, take the right-hand branch (signposted to Hillsford Bridge). Towards the top you will come to another path going sharp right to Lyn Bridge; ignore that and carry straight on to a T-junction. Turn left (signposted to Watersmeet).

❸ About 250 yards beyond the T-junction, you will see a grassy track leading off to the right; take it, passing through a gate, and follow it between field walls. You will soon come to a T-junction; turn left (signposted to Hillsford Bridge) and go through a gate into a field. Go through another gate at the end of the field, onto another grassy track between walls. A third gate leads you into a farmyard; cross it to another gate and cross the field beyond to yet another gate and another track. Two more gates follow, and you then turn left and then right around some houses, following the sign to Hillsford Bridge and Watersmeet. There are two more gates, separated by a track, after the second of which you join another path.

❹ Bear right (signposted to Hillsford Bridge). A little further on you come to a path leading off left, signposted to Watersmeet; take that and follow it

FOOD AND DRINK

The National Trust tearoom at Watersmeet, about halfway along the route, serves a range of wholesome snacks and soups, as well as cream teas, in an idyllic setting by the river, but is only open from April to October. Telephone: 01598 753300. For year-round refreshment, the Rising Sun Hotel in Lynmouth itself takes a lot of beating. Comprising a row of 14th century cottages, it offers bar snacks at midday and a restaurant menu in the evenings in a friendly and welcoming atmosphere. Telephone: 01598 753223.

steeply down the hill into a wood. It crosses an open patch and re-enters the wood, winding steeply down to a road. Cross over to the National Trust car park and go down some steps to another steep path going down towards the East Lyn River.

❺ At the path junction almost opposite the National Trust's tearoom at Watersmeet, turn left, almost back on yourself, and follow the path alongside the river. You pass a bridge on the right; join the track leading from it but, when the track starts to climb left up the hill, branch off onto the path that runs along the riverbank. You cross a drive and come to a footbridge across the river; ignore it and carry straight on, following the sign to Lynmouth. At the fork in the path, keep right (signposted to Lynmouth again). At the next bridge cross over and continue downstream on the other bank. At the next junction go straight on; ignore the next bridge and go straight on to join a road. Follow it until you come to a white bridge on your left; cross it and turn right into the top car park. At the far end, cross the main road and follow Riverside Road back to the bottom car park.

SUGGESTED READING

Bennie, Michael, *Walking Through Dartmoor's Past*, Peninsula Press, 1998

Freeman, Ray, *Dartmouth: A New History of the Port and its People*, Harbour Books, 1983

Goaman, Muriel, *Old Bideford and District*, Cox, 1968

Green, Christina, *Devon Yarns*, Countryside Books, 1995

Hoskins, W.G., *Two Thousand Years in Exeter*, Phillimore, 1963

Hoskins, W.G., *Devon*, Devon Books, 1992

Kendall, H.G., *The Plymouth and Dartmoor Railway*, Oakwood Press, 1968

Norris, Sally, *Tales of Old Devon*, Countryside Books, 1991

Pettit, Paul, *Prehistoric Dartmoor*, Forest Publishing, 1995

Stanes, Robin A., *A History of Devon*, Phillimore, 1986

Toulson, Shirley, *The Companion Guide to Devon*, HarperCollins, 1991